SKILLS DEVELOPMENT

1 It's a wonderful world!

Tenses · Auxiliary verbs · Short answers · What's in a word? · Social expressions

TEST YOUR GRAMMAR

1 Make questions with *you* from the sentences.

1 I come from Scotland. *(Where?)*

> *Where do you come from?*

2 I was born in London in 1984. *(Where? When?)*
3 I live in Milan. *(Where?)*
4 I've got two brothers and a sister. *(How many?)*
5 I'm studying English because I need it for my job. *(Why?)*
6 I've been studying English for three years. *(How long?)*
7 I've been to the United States, Canada, Japan, and Australia. *(Which countries?)*
8 I went to Canada three years ago. *(When?)*

2 Ask and answer the questions with a partner.

> *Where do you come from?*

> *From Mexico.*

> *Where were you born?*

> *In Puebla, a city near Mexico City.*

3 Tell the class about your partner.

Enrique comes from Mexico. He was born in Puebla in 1985, but now he lives in Mexico City.

WHAT DO YOU KNOW?

Tenses and auxiliary verbs

1 Answer the questions in the quiz.

T 1.1 Listen and check.

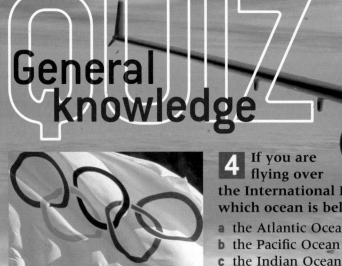

QUIZ

General knowledge

1 When did the modern Olympic Games start?

a 1806   b 1896   c 1922

2 How long does it take for the sun's rays to reach the Earth?

a 8 minutes
b 8 hours
c 8 days

3 What was Neil Armstrong doing when he said in 1969, 'That's one small step for a man, one giant leap for mankind.'?

4 If you are flying over the International Date Line, which ocean is below you?

a the Atlantic Ocean
b the Pacific Ocean
c the Indian Ocean

5 What doesn't a vegetarian eat?

6 What does www. stand for?

7 Where were glasses invented?

a Mexico
b Italy
c China

8 How many times has Brazil won the World Cup?

GRAMMAR SPOT

1 Which questions in the quiz contain the following tenses?

Present Simple	Past Simple	Present Perfect Simple
Present Continuous	Past Continuous	Present Perfect Continuous
Present Simple passive	Past Simple passive	

2 Which tenses use the auxiliary verbs *do/does/did* to make the negative and question?
Which tenses use the auxiliary verb *have*?
Which tenses use the auxiliary verb *be*?

▶▶ **Grammar Reference 1.1–1.3 pp71–72**

2 In groups, write some general knowledge questions. Ask the other groups.

9 **What was John Lennon doing when he was assassinated?**

a performing on stage
b recording an album
c returning to his apartment

10 **Which language is spoken by the most people in the world?**

a Spanish b Chinese c English

11 **Why didn't Nelson Mandela become President of South Africa until he was 76 years old?**

12 **How long have people been sending emails?**

a since the 1960s
b since the 1970s
c since the 1990s

PRACTICE

Negatives and pronunciation

1 Correct the information in the sentences.

1 The sun rises in the west.
2 Cows eat meat.
3 Mercedes-Benz cars are made in Canada.
4 Neil Armstrong landed on the moon in 1989.
5 John Lennon was performing on stage when he was assassinated.
6 The Pyramids were built by the Chinese.
7 We've been in class for five hours.
8 We're studying Italian.

> *The sun doesn't rise in the west! It rises in the east!*

T 1.2 Listen and compare. Notice the stress and intonation. Practise saying the sentences.

Talking about you

2 Complete the questions.

1 A What did you do last night?
  B I stayed at home and watched television.
2 A What kind of books you like reading?
  B Horror stories and science fiction.
3 A _____ ever been to the United States?
  B Yes, I have. I went there last year.
  A _____ like it?
  B Yes, I really enjoyed it.
4 A What _____ the teacher _____?
  B He's helping Maria with this exercise.
5 A _____ your mother do?
  B She works in a bank.
6 A Why _____ do your homework last night?
  B Because I didn't feel well.
7 A What _____ doing next weekend?
  B I'm going to a party.
8 A _____ you _____ a TV in your bedroom?
  B No, I haven't. Just a CD player.

T 1.3 Listen and check. With a partner, ask and answer the questions about you.

is or *has*?

3 **T 1.4** Listen to the sentences. They all contain *'s*. Write *is* or *has*.

1 __is__   3 _____   5 _____   7 _____
2 _____   4 _____   6 _____   8 _____

MAKING CONVERSATION
Short answers

1 **T 1.5** Listen to the breakfast conversation. How does Emma feel?

Dad	Good morning! Did you have a nice time last night?
Emma	Yes.
Dad	Do you want breakfast?
Emma	No.
Dad	Have you had any coffee?
Emma	Yes.
Dad	Is Bill coming round tonight?
Emma	No.
Dad	OK. Are you leaving for school soon?
Emma	Yes. Bye!

2 **T 1.6** Listen to a similar conversation. What are the differences?

3 Complete the conversation.

Dad	Good morning! Did you have a nice time last night?
Emma	Yes, _____. I went round to Bill's house.
Dad	Do you want breakfast?
Emma	No, _____, thanks. I'm not hungry.
Dad	Have you had any coffee?
Emma	Yes, _____. I don't want any more, thanks.
Dad	Is Bill coming round tonight?
Emma	No, _____. He's going out for dinner with his family.
Dad	OK. Are you leaving for school soon?
Emma	Yes, _____. I'm going right now. Bye!

T 1.6 Listen again and check.

4 Close your books. Try to remember the conversation.

GRAMMAR SPOT

1 We use short answers in English conversation because *yes* or *no* on its own can sound impolite. It helps if you can add some information.

> *Did you watch the match last night?*

> *Yes, I did. It was great!*

2 Reply to these questions using a short answer. Add some information.

Do you like cooking?   **No, I don't. But I like eating!**
Have you got any brothers or sisters?
Is it cold out today?
Are you working hard?
Did you go out last night?
Have you ever been to Singapore?

▶▶ **Grammar Reference 1.4 p72**

5 **T 1.7** Listen to the questions. Answer using a short answer, and add some information.

PRACTICE

Conversations

1 Match a question in **A** with a short answer in **B** and a line in **C**.

A	B	C
1 Do you like studying English?	No, I haven't.	It's freezing.
2 Is it a nice day today?	Yes, I am.	It's my favourite subject.
3 Have you seen my pen?	Yes, I do.	I couldn't afford to.
4 Are you staying at home this evening?	No, I didn't.	Do you want to come round?
5 Did you go on holiday last summer?	No, it isn't.	You can borrow mine if you want.

T 1.8 Listen and check. Practise the conversations with a partner.

2 Read the class survey and add two questions of your own. Stand up! Ask three students the questions and complete the chart. Remember to add some information in your reply.

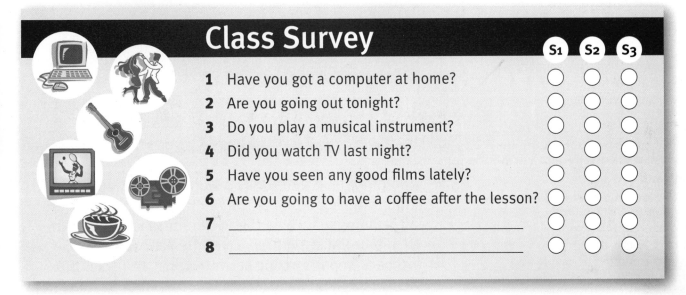

Class Survey

| | S₁ | S₂ | S₃ |

1 Have you got a computer at home?

2 Are you going out tonight?

3 Do you play a musical instrument?

4 Did you watch TV last night?

5 Have you seen any good films lately?

6 Are you going to have a coffee after the lesson?

7 _____

8 _____

Getting information

3 The United Nations invites celebrities from all over the world to be Goodwill Ambassadors. Work with a partner. You each have different information about Kaori Sato, who works for the UN.
Ask and answer questions.

Student A Look at p81.
Student B Look at p82.

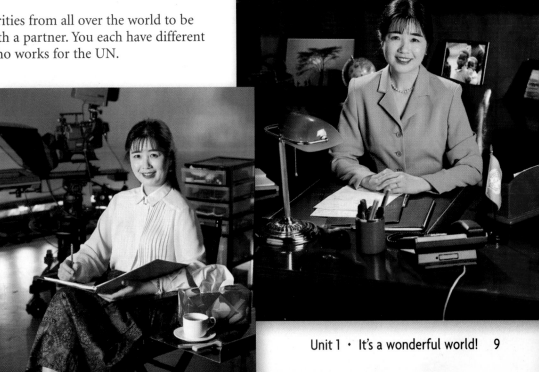

READING AND SPEAKING
Wonders of the modern world

1 Match each topic in **A** with two items in **B**.

A	B
International travel	solar system
	airlines
Medical science	competition
	online
The Internet	corn
	health care
Agriculture	drug abuse
	penicillin
Space travel	famine
	galaxies
The Olympic Games	abroad
	website

2 Read the text about the wonders of the world. Write a topic from **A** in the paragraph headings 1–6.

3 Answer the questions.

1 What has changed because of the Internet? What will happen with the Internet?
2 What has happened in space exploration since 1969?
3 What is the most noticeable result of better health care?
4 **✗** = the number of people who travelled abroad in the nineteenth century. What does **✗** also equal?
5 What are the good and bad things about the Olympics?
6 What point was Jonathan Swift making about farmers and politicians?
7 'We are still here!' Why is this a wonder?
8 What do these numbers refer to?

100 million	a few hundred	1969
millions of people	47 four	1709 50

Talking about you

4 In groups, discuss one of these questions.

- What are your favourite websites?
- When did you last travel by plane? Where were you going?
- Are there any stories about health care in the news at the moment?
- What sporting events are taking place now or in the near future?

WONDERS OF

I don't believe that today's wonders are similar in kind to the wonders of the Ancient World. They were all buildings, such as the Pyramids in Egypt, or other architectural structures. Over the past 100 years, we have seen amazing technological and scientific achievements. These are surely our modern wonders.

1

It is everywhere. More than half a billion people use it, and the number of people who are online increases by 100 million every year. In 1994 there were only a few hundred web pages. Today there are billions.

It has revolutionized the way we live and work. But we are still in the early days. Soon there will be more and more interactivity between the user and the website, and we will be able to give instructions using speech.

2

In 1969, Neil Armstrong stepped out of his space capsule onto the surface of the moon and made his famous statement: 'That's one small step for a man, one giant leap for mankind'. Since then, there have been space probes to Mars, Jupiter, Saturn, and even to the sun. One day, a space observatory will study how the first stars and galaxies began.

So far, it seems that we are alone in the universe. There are no signs yet that there is intelligent life outside our own solar system. But who knows what the future holds?

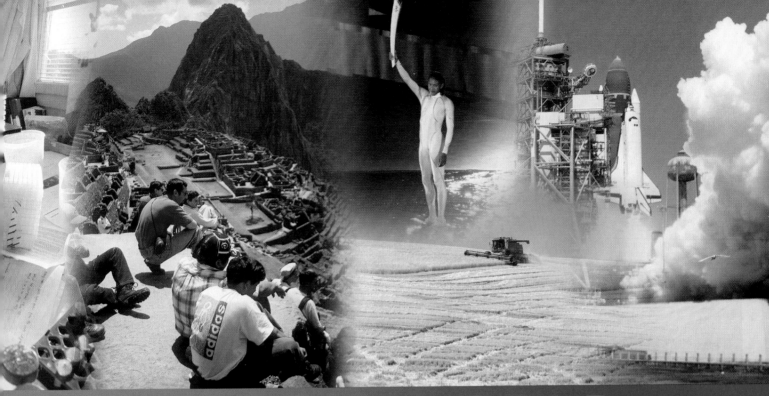

⌐E MODERN WORLD

by Ann Halliday

3

Surely nothing has done more for the comfort and happiness of the human race than the advances in health care! How many millions of people have benefited from the humble aspirin? How many lives has penicillin saved? Average life expectancy worldwide has risen dramatically over the past 100 years, from about 47 years in 1900 to about 77 years today.

4

We are a world on the move. Airlines carry more than 1.5 billion people to their destinations every year. It is estimated that, at any one time these days, there are as many people travelling in aeroplanes as the total number of people who travelled abroad in the whole of the nineteenth century (but I have no idea how they worked this out!).

5

It is true that they are now commercialized, and there is greed and drug abuse. However, it is a competition in which almost every country in the world takes part. Every four years, for a brief moment, we see the world come together in peace and friendship. We feel hope again for the future of mankind.

6

In 1724, Jonathan Swift wrote, 'Whoever makes two blades of grass or two ears of corn grow where only one grew before serves mankind better than the whole race of politicians'. In Europe our farmers have done this. In 1709, whole villages in France died of hunger. Now in Europe, we can't eat all the food we produce. If only politicians could find a way to share it with those parts of the world where there is famine.

7 We are still here!

The last wonder of the modern world is simply that we are still here. We have had nuclear weapons for over 50 years that could destroy the world, but we haven't used them to do it. This is surely the greatest wonder of all.

LISTENING AND SPEAKING
My wonders

1 **T 1.9** Listen to three people from the same family saying what they think are the wonders of the modern world. Complete the chart.

	What is the wonder?	What's good about it?	Are there any problems?
Sam	dishwasher		
Kelly			
Peter			

2 Work with a partner. Which of these inventions do you think is the most important? Mark them ☐ for the most important to ☐ for the least important.

☐ the computer   ☐ nuclear weapons
☐ the car   ☐ the space rocket
☐ the television   ☐ the mobile phone
☐ the aeroplane   ☐ the space satellite

3 Work in groups of four. Work together to agree on the three most important inventions. Which has changed the world the most?

4 Talk together as a class. What other machines, inventions, or discoveries would you add to the list?

VOCABULARY
What's in a word?

These exercises will help you with your vocabulary learning.

Parts of speech and meaning

1 These sentences all contain the nonsense word *uggy*. Is *uggy* used as a verb, an adjective, a noun, or an adverb? How do you know?

1 I couldn't hear the film because the man next to me was eating his *uggy* so loudly.
2 There was a lot of snow on the road. Unfortunately, I *uggied* on some ice and crashed into a tree.
3 When Pierre and Madeleine met, they fell *uggily* in love and got married one month later.
4 After an *uggy* day at work, with meetings and phone calls all day, I was ready for a quiet evening.

Can you guess what *uggy* means in the four sentences?

Which real English word goes in each sentence?

• passionately   • skidded   • hectic   • popcorn

Spelling and pronunciation

2 In these groups three words rhyme, but one is different. Work with a partner and read them aloud. <u>Underline</u> the word in each group which has a different vowel sound.

▶▶ **Phonetic symbols – inside back cover**

1 /ʊ/ or /uː/?   good   food   wood   stood
2 /iː/ or /e/?   bread   head   read (*present*)   read (*past*)
3 /eɪ/ or /e/?   paid   made   played   said
4 /ʌ/ or /əʊ/?   done   phone   sun   won
5 /eə/ or /ɪə/?   dear   hear   bear   near
6 /ɜː/ or /ɔː/?   work   fork   walk   pork

T 1.10 Listen and check. What do you notice about English spelling?

3 Here are some of the words from exercise 2 in phonetic symbols. Read them aloud, then write them.

1 /fuːd/ _____   5 /riːd/ _____
2 /nɪə/ _____   6 /wɜːk/ _____
3 /stʊd/ _____   7 /fəʊn/ _____
4 /peɪd/ _____   8 /wɔːk/ _____

T 1.11 Listen and check.

Word formation

4 Write different forms of the word *act* using the suffixes from the box.

-or	-ion	-ing	-ive	-ivities

1 My brother's an act_____ .
   He's making an advert now.
2 My grandmother is 89, but she's still very act_____ .
3 This is not a time to do nothing. It is a time for act_____.
4 Act_____ is not usually a well-paid job.
5 We do a lot of act_____ in class to learn English.

Words that go together

5 Match a word in **A** with a word in **B**.

A	**B**
strong	carefully
full-time	coffee
film	in love
drive	**a jumper**
fall	star
try on	job

Keeping vocabulary records

6 Do you have a vocabulary notebook? Discuss with your teacher and other students how you record new vocabulary. Which of these do you use?

- the translation
- the part of speech (verb, noun, etc.)
- the meaning (using other words)
- the pronunciation
- an example sentence

hectic (adj) /'hektɪk/ = very busy
   I had a hectic day at the office.
_____
_____
_____

WRITING: Correcting mistakes (1)
 Go to p55

EVERYDAY ENGLISH
Social expressions

1 When we're talking with friends we use a lot of idiomatic expressions.

Hurry up, we're late.

Hang on a sec! I need to go the loo!

Match a line in **A** with a line in **B**.

A	**B**
1 Sorry I'm late. I got stuck in traffic.	That sounds like a good idea. The break will do you good.
2 Bye, Mum! I'm off to school now.	So am I. I can't stand all this rain.
3 Have you heard that Jenny's going out with Pete?	Never mind. You're here now. Come in and sit down.
4 How long did it take you to do the homework?	Ages! How about you?
5 I don't know about you, but I'm sick and tired of this weather.	Yes, it cost a fortune!
6 Who was that I saw you with last night?	Really? I don't know what she sees in him!
7 I'm tired. I'm taking next week off.	I'm sorry. I can't make it then. What about a bit later?
8 Let's go for a run in the park!	Take care, my love. Have a nice day!
9 Can we get together this afternoon at 3.00?	Me? Run? You must be joking!
10 What a gorgeous coat! Was it expensive?	Mind your own business!

T 1.12 Listen and check. Practise the conversations with a partner.

2 **T 1.13** Listen to the sentences. Reply using a line from **B** in exercise 1. Make any necessary changes.

3 Choose some of the conversations from exercise 1 and continue them.

   A What a gorgeous coat! Was it expensive?
   B Yes, it cost a fortune. But the material's beautiful, don't you think?
   A Wow! Where did you get it?
   B I saw it in the window of that new shop in the High Street, you know, it's called 'Chic'.
   A Yes, I know it. They have some really nice stuff.

2 Get happy!

TEST YOUR GRAMMAR

Look at the pairs of sentences.
Which one is correct? Why?

1 They have a teenage son.
   They're having a teenage son.

2 She speaks five languages.
   She's speaking five languages.

3 Don't turn off the TV! I watch it.
   Don't turn off the TV! I'm watching it.

4 Oh no! It rains.
   Oh no! It's raining.

5 We're thinking opera is boring.
   We think opera is boring.

6 English speaks all over the world.
   English is spoken all over the world.

WHAT MAKES PEOPLE HAPPY?
Present tenses

1 Look at the ingredients for happiness. How important is each one
   to you? **1** = very important; **5** = not important.

☐ good health in mind and body
☐ job satisfaction
☐ a loving marriage
☐ hobbies and leisure activities
☐ no money worries

☐ a big house
☐ regular holidays
☐ a supportive family
☐ lots of friends

Compare your answers with a partner.

2 What do you think is the happiest time of a person's life –
   when they are young or when they are old? Why?

3 **T 2.1** Read and listen to the text about Sidney Fisk. Answer the questions.

1 What do you think are the good and bad things about Sidney's life?
2 Do you think his life is exciting or boring? Would you like to have a life like Sidney's?
3 Do you know any people with similar lives? Are they happy?

'I don't know if I'm happy.'

Sidney Fisk, 45

Work

Sidney Fisk is a lawyer. He's paid very well, but he usually has to work long hours. He works for an international company in Dallas, Texas, so he travels a lot in his job. At the moment he's working in Mexico, and next week he's travelling to France.

Home life

Sidney is married and he's got two children, aged 11 and 14. He rarely sees his children because so much of his time is spent away from home. He's got a beautiful house in a suburb of Dallas. It's very big, with eight bedrooms. His wife is an interior designer.

Free time

If he's at home at the weekend, he and his wife sometimes play golf, but that doesn't happen very often. They never have much time to relax together.

Is he happy?

He says he doesn't know if he's happy. He's too busy to think about it.

GRAMMAR SPOT

1 Find these words in the text about Sidney Fisk: *usually, often, rarely, never*. What kind of words are they?

2 What tense are most of the verbs in the text? Why?

3 Find two examples each in the text of the Present Continuous and the Present Simple passive. Which auxiliary verb is used to form these?

4 Complete the questions and answers with the correct auxiliary verbs.

a _____ he travel a lot?   Yes, he _____.
b _____ she work in a bank?   No, she _____.
c _____ they play golf?   Yes, they _____.
d _____ you play tennis?   No, I _____.
e _____ he paid a lot?   Yes, he _____.
f _____ he working in France at the moment?   No, he _____.

▶▶ Grammar Reference 2.1 and 2.2 pp72–73

---

4 Complete the questions about Sidney. Then ask and answer them with a partner.

- . . . married?
- What . . . do?
- Where . . . live?
- Has . . . any children?
- What . . . his wife do?
- Which sports . . . play?
- Where . . . working at the moment?
- . . . paid very well?

Is he married?

Yes, he is.

T 2.2 Listen and check.

5 Ask and answer similar questions with your partner.

Are you married?

No, I'm not.

Have you got any brothers or sisters?

PRACTICE

Listening and speaking

1 **T 2.3** Look at the photos and listen to Jeff Norman. What's unusual about his lifestyle? What does he like about it?

Extra! Extra! Read all about it! 45-year-old college graduate makes $60,000 a year as a paperboy!

JEFF NORMAN **from Iowa City, Iowa**

---

2 What did Jeff say? Complete the sentences.

1 I ___'m___ ___paid___ good money – $60,000 a year. And I often _____ $50 a week in tips.

2 I _____ _____ at 2.00 a.m. The first newspaper _____ _____ at 2.30 a.m.

3 I _____ a red Chevy Blazer and the newspapers _____ _____ into the back.

4 I _____ the peace and quiet.

5 Occasionally, I _____ a jogger.

6 I usually _____ _____ home by 7.00 a.m.

7 My wife _____ at the University of Iowa.

8 Some days I _____ my kids' baseball team, other days I _____ golf.

9 I _____ also _____ for my master's degree at the moment.
I _____ _____ be a marriage counsellor.

10 Some people _____ it's not much of a job, but, hey, when they _____ _____ in an office, I _____ _____ golf.

T 2.4 Listen and check.

3 Write notes about Sidney and Jeff in the chart.

	Sidney Fisk	Jeff Norman
Work		
Home and family		
Free time		

Work with a partner. Compare Sidney's life with Jeff's. How old are they? How many things do they have in common? Who do you think is happier? Why?

WHAT DO YOU DO?

Simple or continuous?

1 **T 2.5** Read and listen to the conversation.

A What do you do?
B I'm an interior designer. I decorate people's homes and give them ideas for furniture and lighting.
A And what are you working on these days?
B Well, I'm not working on a home at the moment. I'm working on a hotel. I'm designing a new lobby for the Plaza.
A Do you like your job?
B Yes, I love it.

Memorize the conversation and practise it with a partner.

2 Work with a partner. Have similar conversations with some of these jobs.

an architect   a research scientist   an artist   an actor
a rock musician   a web page designer   a journalist
a film director   a football player   a zookeeper

3 Ask each other about your own jobs or studies.

GRAMMAR SPOT

1 Some verbs are used in both simple and continuous forms. These are called **action verbs**.

> She usually **drives** to work, but today she **isn't driving**. She's **walking**.

2 Some verbs are almost never used in the continuous form. These are called **state verbs**.

> I **like** black coffee. (NOT ~~I'm liking~~ black coffee.)

3 Seven of these verbs are *not* usually used in the Present Continuous. <u>Underline</u> them.

<u>like</u>   know   understand   work   enjoy   think (= opinion)
come   play   have (= possession)   love   want

▶▶ **Grammar Reference 2.3 p73**

PRACTICE

Discussing grammar

1 Are these sentences correct (✓) or incorrect (✗)? Correct the mistakes.

1 What do you want to drink? ✓
2 I'm not understanding this word. ✗
   I don't understand this word.
3 I'm loving you a lot.
4 Do you think Michiko plays golf well?
5 I'm sorry. I'm not knowing the answer.
6 We're enjoying the lesson very much. We're working hard.
7 I'm thinking you speak English very well.
8 The lions are fed once a day. They're being fed at the moment.

2 Complete the pairs of sentences using the verb in the Present Simple or the Present Continuous.

1 come
   Alec and Marie are French. They _____ from Paris.
   They'll be here very soon. They _____ by car.

2 have
   Lisa can't come to the phone. She _____ dinner now.
   She _____ a beautiful new car.

3 think
   I _____ that all politicians tell lies.
   I _____ about my girlfriend at the moment. She's in Australia.

4 not enjoy
   We _____ this party at all. The music is too loud.
   We _____ big parties.

5 watch
   Be quiet! I _____ my favourite programme.
   I always _____ it on Thursday evenings.

6 see
   Joe isn't here. He _____ the doctor at the moment.
   I _____ your problem, but I can't help you. I'm sorry.

7 use (Careful!)
   This room _____ usually _____ for big meetings.
   But today it _____ being _____ for a party.

READING AND SPEAKING
I'm a clown doctor!

1 What does a doctor do? What does a clown do? Write down three things for each. Tell the class your ideas.

2 Which of these things did you think of? Which do clowns do? Which do doctors do? Which do both do?

wear funny clothes	wear white coats
make children feel better	do magic tricks
perform operations	give injections
wear red rubber noses	make funny faces
tell jokes	give medicine

3 Look at the pictures. Lucy Cheetham is a clown doctor working for *Theodora Children's Trust* – a charitable organization. What do you think a clown doctor does?

4 Read the introduction. What is the new kind of medicine?

5 Read the rest of the article. Answer the questions.
1 Who is Dr LooLoo? Who is Dr Chequers?
2 In what ways is their job 'extremely silly'? Give examples.
3 How did Lucy become a Theodora clown doctor?
4 Why does she like her job?
5 What does she wear?
6 What would be useless?
7 Why is it useful to eat in the hospital cafeteria?
8 What does she do after work?
9 Where does the money for Lucy's salary come from?
10 Describe a typical working day for Lucy.

She arrives in the hospital with ...
Then she goes into the wards and ...

GRAMMAR SPOT

1 Complete these sentences from the text.
All over the world, children in hospital _____ _____ _____ with a new kind of medicine.
It's a charity; so we _____ _____ with the money people give.
What tenses are they?

2 Complete these passive sentences.
1 People of all ages love clowns.
   Clowns _____ _____ by people of all ages.
2 He is giving her an injection.
   She's _____ given an injection.

▶▶ **Grammar Reference 2.4 p74**

THE CLOWN DOCTOR

All over the world, children in hospital are being treated with a new kind of medicine: laughter. **LUCY** is 23 and works for *Theodora Children's Trust*. She is one of many clown doctors who bring a smile to the faces of sick children.

I'm a Theodora clown doctor, I call myself Dr LooLoo. I spend two days a week in children's hospitals being extremely silly with my friend and colleague Dr Chequers. We make funny faces, tell jokes, and do magic tricks. As I walk into the wards I blow bubbles, shake hands with the kids, and make up nonsense songs for those children well enough to sing. We take special balloons to make 'balloon animals' and tell funny stories about them. We often meet kids who one week look really sick, then we go back the next week and they're racing about yelling 'Hi there, Dr LooLoo! Hi Dr Chequers!'

I'm naturally a very cheerful person. I've always been a clown. In fact my father's a clown and I started working with him when I was eight years old. I knew it was just the job for me and I became a clown doctor because I think it's a great way to cheer up sick, frightened children in hospital. I wear a fancy coat, a yellow shirt, and tights with big stripes. Also, I have a red rubber nose and wear my hair in crazy plaits.

Being a clown in a hospital is very tiring both physically and emotionally. We have to learn not to show our feelings, otherwise we'd be useless. Clown doctors are sensitive but this is not a side most people see. To the children we're happy all the time. I'm still learning to allow myself to feel sad occasionally. There are special kids you get really close to. At the

moment I'm working with a very sick little girl from Bosnia who speaks no English, so our only common language is laughter. She's been in and out of hospital for operations so many times and she's always on my mind.

At lunchtime we eat in the hospital cafeteria and that's really useful because we meet the nurses and doctors. They tell us about particular kids who they think will benefit from a clown doctor visit. If a child is frightened, perhaps they're being given an injection or some nasty medicine – we can distract them so the nurses can do their job.

About six o'clock Dr Chequers and I take off our make-up and change our clothes. We're totally exhausted. Sometimes I have a night out with friends, it helps me unwind. When I finally fall into bed, I crash out. At weekends we are often asked to participate in events to raise money for *Theodora Children's Trust*. It's a charity; so we are paid with the money people give. Being a clown doctor makes the worries of everyday life seem small. All in all, I feel privileged to do this job.

Language work

6 Find lines in the text which mean the same as the following.

1 They're running about shouting.
2 I have a happy personality.
3 We would be no help at all.
4 I'm always thinking about her.
5 I go out for the evening with friends.
6 It helps me relax.
7 I go to bed and immediately fall into a deep sleep.
8 I am lucky to have this job.

7 Read the interview with Lucy (L). Complete the interviewer's (I) questions.

I _____?
L Oh yes, I do. I enjoy my job very much.
I _____?
L Because I love working with children and making them laugh.
I _____?
L I wear crazy clothes. A fancy coat and stripy tights.
I _____?
L Well, at the moment I'm working with a very sick little girl from Bosnia. She's had so many operations. She's very special to me.
I _____?
L No, she doesn't. We communicate through laughter.
I _____?
L Yes, it is. It's very tiring indeed. I'm exhausted at the end of each day.
I _____?
L No, I don't. I often go out with friends. I have the best friends and the best job in the world.

T 2.6 Listen and compare your answers. Are your questions exactly the same? What are the differences?

What do you think?

Discuss the questions in groups.

- What are some of the good and bad points about being a clown doctor?
- What kind of jobs make people happiest?
- When are you happiest? At work? At home? With friends?
- What were your happiest times last year?
- It's often said 'laughter is the best medicine'. Do you agree?

VOCABULARY AND LISTENING
Sport and leisure

1 Make a list of as many sports and leisure activities as you can think of. Use the pictures to help you.

2 Write *play*, *go*, or *do*.

_____ snowboarding	_____ aerobics	_____ volleyball	_____ fishing	_____ golf
_____ jogging	_____ basketball	_____ football	_____ yoga	_____ mountain biking

3 Choose some of the sports or leisure activities from your list and complete the chart. Use a dictionary to look up any new words that you need.

Sport / Activity	People	Place	Equipment and clothes
go snowboarding	snowboarder	ski resort / dry ski slope	snowboard / boots / helmet / goggles / waterproof jacket and trousers

4 **T 2.7** Listen to three people talking about a sport or activity they enjoy and take notes.

	Mary	Jenny	Thomas
Which sport / activity are they talking about?			
How often do they do it?			
Where do they do it?			
What equipment and clothes do they need?			
Are they good at it?			

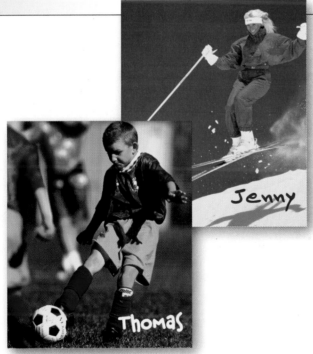

5 Ask and answer questions with a partner.

- What sports do you play?
- How often . . . ?
- Where . . . ?
- What equipment . . . ?
- Are you good at . . . ?

WRITING: Letters and emails
▶▶ Go to p56

EVERYDAY ENGLISH
Numbers and dates

1 Say the numbers.

15 **50** **406** **72** **128**

90 **19** **850** **36** **1,520**

247 **5,000** **100,000** **2,000,000**

T 2.8 Listen and practise.

2 Say the numbers.

Money
£400   50p   €9.40   €47.99   ¥5,000 $100

Fractions
¼   ¾   ⅔   ⅞   12½

Decimals and percentages
6.2   17.25   50%   75.7%   100%

Dates
1995   **2020**   1789   **15/7/94**   30/10/02

Phone numbers
01865-556890   **800 451-7545**   919 677-1303

T 2.9 Listen and practise.

3 **T 2.10** Listen to the conversations. Write the numbers you hear.

1 <u>fifteenth</u> _____
2 _____ _____
3 _____ _____
   ☐☐☐☐ ☐☐☐☐ ☐☐☐☐ ☐☐☐☐
4 _____ _____
5 _____ _____

Discuss what each number refers to with a partner.
The 15th is a date.

4 Work with a partner. Write five numbers that are important in your life and explain why.

3 Telling tales

Past tenses · Passive · Art and literature · Giving opinions

TEST YOUR GRAMMAR

Match the sentences and pictures.

1 When Carol arrived home, Mark cooked dinner.
2 When Carol arrived home, Mark was cooking dinner.
3 When Carol arrived home, Mark had cooked dinner.

What is the difference in meaning?

a

b

c

A NATIVE AMERICAN FOLK TALE
Past tenses

1 Look at the pictures. They tell the story of Gluskap, a warrior from the Algonquian tribe of North America. What can you see? What do you think the story is about?

2 Read the story on p23 and the phrases below. Complete the story with the phrases.
   a had run a few miles
   b had fought and won so many battles
   c was still screaming
   d had never heard such a terrible noise
   e was sitting and sucking a piece of sugar
   f had never heard of Wasis

   T 3.1 Listen and check. What do you think is the moral of the story?

GRAMMAR SPOT

1 Which tense is used in these two sentences? Which verbs are regular? Which are irregular?

He **laughed** and **went** up to the baby.
He **danced** and **sang**.

Find more examples in the story and underline them.

2 What are the tenses in these sentences? What is the difference in meaning?

He **laughed** when he **saw** the baby.
He **was laughing** when he **saw** the baby.
He **laughed** when he**'d seen** the baby. (he'd = he had)

3 Find two examples of the Past Simple passive in the story.

▶▶ **Grammar Reference 3.1–3.4 pp74–76**

3 Work with a partner. Write the verbs from the box in the chart according to the pronunciation of the *-ed* ending.

| ~~laughed~~ covered wanted stopped shouted listened |
| opened boasted looked danced screamed pointed |

/t/	/d/	/ɪd/
laughed		

T 3.2 Listen, check, and practise.

THE TALE OF GLUSKAP AND THE BABY

Gluskap the warrior was very pleased with himself because he (1)___. He boasted to a woman friend: 'Nobody can beat me!'

'Really?' said the woman. 'I know someone who can beat you. His name is Wasis.' Gluskap (2)___. He immediately wanted to meet him and fight him. So he was taken to the woman's village. The woman pointed to a baby who (3)___ on the floor of a teepee.

'There,' she said. 'That is Wasis. He is little, but he is very strong.' Gluskap laughed and went up to the baby. 'I am

Gluskap. Fight me!' he shouted. Little Wasis looked at him for a moment, then he opened his mouth. 'Waaah! Waaah!' he screamed. Gluskap (4)___. He danced a war dance and sang some war songs. Wasis screamed louder. 'Waaah! Waaah! Waaah!' Gluskap covered his ears and ran out of the teepee. After he (5)___, he stopped and listened. The baby (6)___. Gluskap the fearless was terrified. He ran on and was never seen again in the woman's village.

PRACTICE

What was she doing?

1 Judy works for MicroSmart Computers in London. Read about what she did yesterday.

microsmart
COMPUTERS

6.30	got up
6.45 – 7.15	packed her suitcase
7.30 – 8.30	drove to the airport
9.20 – 10.15	flew to Glasgow
11.00 – 12.45	had a meeting
1.00 – 2.15	had lunch
2.30 – 4.15	visited Dot Com Enterprises
5.30 – 6.15	wrote a report on the plane
8.00 – 8.45	put the baby to bed
9.00 – 11.00	relaxed and listened to music

2 Work with a partner. Ask and answer questions about what Judy was doing at these times.

7.00 a.m.	8.00 a.m.	10.00 a.m.	11.30 a.m.
1.30 p.m.	3.00 p.m.	6.00 p.m.	8.30 p.m.	10.00 p.m.

T 3.3 Listen and check.

> *What was she doing at 7 o'clock yesterday morning?*

> *She was packing her suitcase.*

3 Write a similar list about what you did yesterday. Ask and answer questions with your partner.

> *What were you doing at 7 o'clock yesterday morning?*

> *I was having a shower.*

Had you heard it before?

4 Work with a partner.

Student A Read a statement from your box.
Student B Answer with the correct response from your box.

STUDENT A
1 I didn't laugh at his joke.
2 Were you surprised by the ending of the film?
3 I went to the airport, but I couldn't get on the plane.
4 I was homesick the whole time I was living in France.
5 The hotel where we stayed on holiday was awful!
6 I met my girlfriend's parents for the first time last Sunday.
7 My grandfather had two sons from his first marriage.

STUDENT B
Why? Had you left your passport at home?
Why? Had you heard it before?
That's a pity. Hadn't you stayed there before?
Really? I didn't know he'd been married before.
Really? I thought you'd met them before.
No, I'd read the book, so I already knew the story.
That's really sad! Had you never lived abroad before?

T 3.4 Listen and check, then listen and repeat.

5 Choose two of the conversations and continue them.

> *I didn't laugh at his joke.*

> *Why? Had you heard it before?*

> *No, I hadn't. I just didn't think it was very funny, that's all.*

> *Really? I thought it was hilarious!*

An amazing thing happened!

6 Wanda and Roy had an amazing story to tell about their holiday. Work with a partner.

Student A Look at p81.
Student B Look at p82.

7 Wanda is telling a friend, Nicola, what happened. Work with a partner. One of you is Wanda and the other is Nicola. Continue their conversation.

> **N** Hi, Wanda. Did you have a good holiday?
> **W** Oh, yeah, we had a great time. But I have to tell you – the most *amazing* thing happened!
> **N** Really? What was that?
> **W** Well, Roy and I were at the beach …

T 3.5 Listen and compare.

Discussing grammar

8 Complete the sentences. Check your answers with a partner. Discuss the differences in meaning.

1 When I arrived at the barbecue, they _____ eating sausages.

   When I arrived at the barbecue, they _____ eaten all the sausages.

2 We thanked our teacher for everything she _____ doing to help us pass the test.

   We thanked our teacher for everything she _____ done to help us pass the test.

3 He told me that they _____ staying at the Carlton Hotel.

   He told me that they _____ stayed at the Carlton Hotel before.

4 _____ you learn Italian when you went to Italy?

   _____ you already learned Italian when you went to Italy?

5 _____ Shakespeare write *Hamlet*?

   _____ *Hamlet* written by Shakespeare?

> **WRITING:** A narrative (1)
> ▶▶ Go to p58

VOCABULARY
Art and literature

1 Write these nouns in the correct column. Which noun goes in both columns?

> painter author poet poem sculpture novel
> picture brush palette chapter biography
> exhibition fairy tale portrait play art gallery
> masterpiece novelist sketch act

ART	LITERATURE

2 Which of these verbs can go with the nouns in exercise 1?

> read write paint draw go to

Read a poem, read a novel …

3 Complete the sentences.

1 Shakespeare _____ many famous _____ and poems.

2 I couldn't put the book down until I'd _____ the last _____.

3 I love _____ about the lives of famous people so I always buy _____.

4 _____ often begin with the words 'Once upon a time'.

5 My friend's a great artist. He _____ my _____ and it looked just like me.

6 He _____ a quick _____ of the trees.

7 We _____ an _____ of Picasso's paintings and sculptures.

READING AND SPEAKING
The painter and the writer

1 Who are or were the most famous painters and writers in your country?

2 You are going to read about the lives of Pablo Picasso and Ernest Hemingway. Discuss these questions.

- Why are they famous?
- What nationality were they?
- Which century were they born in?
- Do you know the names of any of their works?
- Do you know anything about their lives?

3 The sentences below appear in the texts. Try to guess which sentences go with which man. Write **P** (Picasso) or **H** (Hemingway).

1 ☐ His first word was *lápiz* (Spanish for *pencil*) and he could draw before he could talk.

2 ☐ He had wanted to become a soldier, but couldn't because he had poor eyesight.

3 ☐ His portraits of people were often made up of triangles and squares with their features in the wrong places.

4 ☐ In the 1930s, he became a war correspondent in the Spanish Civil War and World War II.

5 ☐ He was awarded the Nobel Prize for literature, but he was too ill to receive it in person.

6 ☐ At the age of 90 he was honoured by an exhibition in the Louvre in Paris.

4 Work in two groups.

Group A Read about Pablo Picasso.
Group B Read about Ernest Hemingway.

Check your answers to exercises 2 and 3.

PABLO PICASSO

The painter

HIS EARLY LIFE

On 25 October, 1881, a baby boy was born in Málaga, Spain. It was a difficult birth and to help him breathe, cigar smoke was blown into his nose! This baby grew up to be one of the twentieth century's greatest painters – **PABLO PICASSO**.

Picasso showed his genius from a very young age. His first word was *lápiz* (Spanish for *pencil*) and he could draw before he could talk. He was the only son in the family, so he was thoroughly spoiled. He hated school and often refused to go unless he was allowed to take one of his father's pet pigeons with him!

Apart from pigeons, his great love was art. When in 1891 his father got a job as an art teacher, Pablo went with him to work and watched him paint. Sometimes he was allowed to help. One evening, his father was painting a picture of their pigeons when he had to leave the room. When he returned, Pablo had completed the picture. It was so beautiful and lifelike that he gave his son his palette and brushes and never painted again. Pablo was just thirteen.

HIS LIFE AS AN ARTIST

His genius as an artist was soon recognized by many people, but others were shocked by his strange and powerful paintings. He is probably best known for his Cubist pictures. His portraits of people were often made up of triangles and squares with their features in the wrong places. One of his most famous portraits was of the American writer Gertrude Stein, who he met after he'd moved to Paris in 1904.

His work changed ideas about art around the world, and to millions of people, modern art means the work of Picasso. *Guernica* [below], which he painted in 1937, records the bombing of that small Basque town during the Spanish Civil War, and is undoubtedly one of the masterpieces of modern painting.

HIS FINAL YEARS

Picasso married twice and also had many mistresses. He had four children. The last, Paloma, was born in 1949 when he was 68 years old. At the age of 90 he was honoured by an exhibition in the Louvre in Paris. He was the first living artist to be shown there.

Picasso created over 6,000 paintings, drawings, and sculptures. Today, a Picasso costs millions of pounds. Once, when the French Minister of Culture was visiting Picasso, the artist accidentally spilled some paint on the Minister's trousers. Picasso apologized and wanted to pay for them to be cleaned, but the Minister said, 'Non! Please, Monsieur Picasso, just sign my trousers!'

Picasso died of heart failure during an attack of influenza in 1973.

Guernica

ERNEST HEMINGWAY
The writer

HIS EARLY LIFE

ERNEST HEMINGWAY was one of the great American writers of the twentieth century. He was born on 21 July 1899, in Oak Park, Illinois, the second of six children. His family was strict and very religious. His father taught his children a love of nature and the outdoor life. Ernest caught his first fish at the age of three, and was given a shotgun for his twelfth birthday. His mother taught him a love of music and art. At school, he was good at English and wrote for the school newspaper. He graduated in 1917, but he didn't go to college. He went to Kansas City and worked as a journalist for the *Star* newspaper. He learned a lot, but left after only six months to go to war.

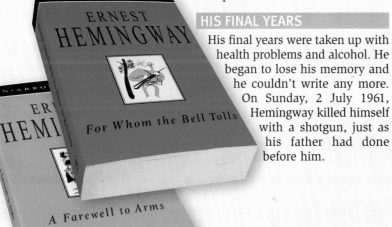

HEMINGWAY AND WAR

Hemingway was fascinated by war. He had wanted to become a soldier, but couldn't because he had poor eyesight. Instead, in the First World War, he became an ambulance driver and was sent to Italy, where he was wounded in 1918. After the war, he went to live in Paris, where he was encouraged in his work by the American writer Gertrude Stein. In the 1930s, he became a war correspondent in the Spanish Civil War and World War II. Many of his books were about war. His most successful book, *For Whom the Bell Tolls*, was written in 1940 and is about the Spanish Civil War. Another novel, *A Farewell to Arms*, is about the futility of war.

HIS PERSONAL LIFE

Hemingway's success in writing was not mirrored by similar success in his personal life. He married four times. His first wife divorced him in 1927. He immediately married again and moved to Key West, Florida, where he enjoyed hunting, fishing, and drinking, but he also suffered from depression. This wasn't helped when, in 1928, his father committed suicide. Hemingway's health was not good and he had many accidents. Two more marriages failed and he began to drink heavily. In 1954, he survived two plane crashes. In October of the same year he was awarded the Nobel Prize for literature, but he was too ill to receive it in person.

HIS FINAL YEARS

His final years were taken up with health problems and alcohol. He began to lose his memory and he couldn't write any more. On Sunday, 2 July 1961, Hemingway killed himself with a shotgun, just as his father had done before him.

---

5 Answer the questions about your person.
   1 Where and when was he born? When and how did he die?
   2 Did he have a happy family life?
   3 How did his parents play a part in his career?
   4 What do you think were the most important events in his early life?
   5 When did he move to Paris? Who did he meet there?
   6 How did war play a part in his life?
   7 How many times was he married?
   8 Which of these dates relate to your person? What do they refer to?

1891	1917	1918	1927	1928
1937	1940	1949	1954	

6 Find a partner from the other group and go through the questions in exercise 5. What similarities and differences can you find between the two men?

   They were both born in the nineteenth century. Picasso was spoiled, but Hemingway's parents were strict.

GRAMMAR SPOT

1 What tense are these verbs?

   Guernica **was painted** by Pablo Picasso.

   A Farewell to Arms and *For Whom the Bell Tolls* **were written** by Ernest Hemingway.

   Find more examples in the texts and underline them.

2 Complete the sentences with the auxiliaries *was*, *were*, or *had*.
   a Pablo's father left the room. When he returned, Pablo _____ completed the picture.
   b Picasso _____ given his father's palette and brushes.
   c Both Hemingway and Picasso _____ living in Paris when they met Gertrude Stein.
   d Both men _____ honoured in their lifetime.

   ►► **Grammar Reference 3.5 p76**

LISTENING AND WRITING
Books and films

1 Work in groups. Do you have a favourite book or film? Why do you like it? Tell your group.

2 Look at the list of books and films. Which do you know? Which are both book *and* film?

- ☐ Dracula
- ☐ Frankenstein
- ☐ Spiderman
- ☐ Harry Potter and the Philosopher's Stone
- ☐ The Silence of the Lambs
- ☐ Titanic
- ☐ Captain Corelli's Mandolin
- ☐ The Godfather
- ☐ Star Wars
- ☐ The Lord of the Rings
- ☐ The Sun Also Rises

3 **T 3.6** Listen to four friends chatting about their favourite books and films. Tick (✓) the titles they mention in exercise 2. What do they say about them? Discuss with your group, then with the class.

4 Write some notes about a book or film that you know and like. Use these questions to help you. Discuss your notes with a partner.

- What's it called?
- Who wrote it?
- Who directed it?
- Who starred in it?
- Who are the main characters?
- Where does it take place?
- What's it about?
- Why do you like it?

5 Use your notes to write a paragraph about the book or film that you chose.

EVERYDAY ENGLISH
Giving opinions

1 What do the <u>underlined</u> words refer to in these sentences?

a <u>It</u> was really boring! I fell asleep during the first act.
   a play

b I didn't like his first <u>one</u>, but I couldn't put his latest one down until the last page.

c <u>It</u> was excellent. Have you seen it yet? It stars Julia Kershaw and Antonio Bellini.

d <u>She</u>'s usually good, but I don't think she was right for this part.

e I think they spoil <u>them</u>. They always give them whatever they want.

f <u>It</u> was a nice break, but the weather wasn't very good.

g <u>They</u> were delicious. John had tomato and mozzarella and I had tuna and sweetcorn.

h <u>It</u> was really exciting, especially when David Stuart scored in the closing minutes.

2 Match questions 1–8 with the opinions in exercise 1.

1 Did you like the film?   `c`
2 What did you think of the play?   ☐
3 Did you like your pizzas?   ☐
4 Do you like Malcolm Baker's novels?   ☐
5 What do you think of their children?   ☐
6 What was your holiday like?   `f`
7 What did you think of Sally Cotter?   `d`
8 What was the match like?   `h`

T 3.7 Listen and check. Practise the questions and answers with a partner.

3 Write down some things you did, places you went to, and people you met last week. Work with a partner and ask for and give opinions about them.

> *I went to a party.*

> *Really? What was it like?*

> *Great! I really enjoyed it.*

> *I met Maria's sister.*

> *What did you think of her?*

> *She's really nice. I liked her a lot.*

4 Doing the right thing

Modal verbs 1 – obligation and permission · Nationality words · Requests and offers

TEST YOUR GRAMMAR

Look at the sentences.

I	can should must have to	go.

1 Write the negatives.
2 Write the questions.
3 Write the third person singular.
4 Which verb is different?

I'm sorry, but I have to go now.

TEENAGERS AND PARENTS
have (got) to, can, and *be allowed to*

1 **T 4.1** Listen to Sarah and Lindsay, aged 14 and 15. What are some of the things they like and don't like about being a teenager?

2 Complete the sentences.

1 You _____ go to work.
2 You _____ pay bills.
3 You _____ go out with your friends.
4 I always _____ tell my mum and dad where I'm going.
5 What time _____ get back home?
6 You _____ buy whatever you want.
7 Adults _____ worry about paying the bills.
8 They _____ always do what they want.
9 We _____ bring mobile phones to class.
10 I _____ go. I _____ do my homework.

T 4.2 Listen and check. Practise saying the sentences.

3 Lindsay talks about her parents. What are some of the things they *have to* do and *don't have to* do?

Her mother has to ...
Her father ...

PRACTICE

Discussing grammar

1 Put these sentences into the negative, the question, and the past.

   1 Henry can swim.
      Henry can't swim.   Can Henry swim?   Henry could swim.
   2 I have to wear a uniform.
   3 She has to work hard.
   4 He can do what he likes.
   5 We're allowed to wear jeans.

Talking about you

2 Look at the chart. Make true sentences about you and your family.

I don't have to do the cooking.

A	B	C
I My parents My mother My father My sister My brother My grandparents My husband/wife	have to has to don't have to doesn't have to had to didn't have to	go to work. get up early. go shopping. clean my room. do the cooking. take out the rubbish. do the washing. do the washing-up.

Compare your sentences with a partner.

3 Complete the sentences with *'ve got to/'s got to* and a line from **C** in exercise 2.

   1 Where's my briefcase? I _____.
   2 Look at those dirty plates! We _____.
   3 Pamela and Charles don't have any food in their house. They _____.
   4 John needs to get an alarm clock. He _____ tomorrow.
   5 I haven't got any clean socks. I _____.
   6 The chef's ill, so the waiter _____.

   T 4.3 Listen and check. Practise saying the sentences.

4 Work in groups. Talk about your school.

   • Are/Were your teachers strict?
   • What are/were you allowed to do?
   • What aren't/weren't you allowed to do?

Signs

5 What do these signs mean? Use *have to/don't have to, can/can't*, or *(not) be allowed to*.

What do you think?

Is it the same in your country?

In Britain ...

• you can get married when you're 16.
• you can't drink alcohol until you're 18.
• you have to wear a seat-belt in a car.
• you can vote when you're 18.
• young people don't have to do military service.
• there are lots of public places where you aren't allowed to smoke.

PLANNING A TRIP
should **and** *must*

1 **T 4.4** Antony and his friend George are going to travel around Asia. Listen to them talking about their trip. What two decisions do they make?

2 Practise the conversation.

A I can't stop thinking about this trip.
G Same here. I spend all my time just looking at maps.
A What do you think? Should we take cash or traveller's cheques?
G I think we should take traveller's cheques. It'll be safer.
A Yeah, I think you're right.
G When should we go to Thailand?
A Well, I don't think we should go during the rainy season. I'd rather go in February or March, when it's drier.
G Sounds like a good idea to me. I can't wait to get going!

3 Match a line in **A** with a sentence in **B** to make more suggestions. Use *I think/don't think we should …*

I think we should buy some guidebooks. They'll give us a lot of information.

A	B
1 … buy some guidebooks.	Our bags will be too heavy to carry.
2 … take plenty of suncream.	I have some friends there.
3 … pack too many clothes.	We don't want to get ill.
4 … take anything valuable.	It'll be really hot.
5 … go to Japan first.	That would be really stupid.
6 … go anywhere dangerous.	They'll give us a lot of information.
7 … have some vaccinations.	We might lose it.

4 **T 4.5** Listen to Antony and his grandmother. She is worried about the boys' trip.

Grandmother	You must write to us every week!
Antony	Yes, I will.
Grandmother	You mustn't lose your passport!
Antony	No, I won't.

Work with a partner. Make similar conversations between Antony and his grandmother. Use the prompts and *must /mustn't*.

- look after your money
- talk to strangers
- go out when it's dark
- drink too much beer
- make sure you eat well
- have a bath regularly
- phone us if you're in trouble
- go anywhere that's dangerous

T 4.6 Listen and check.

GRAMMAR SPOT

1 Look at the sentences below.

  We **should** take traveller's cheques.
  You **must** look after your money.

  Which sentence expresses strong obligation?
  Which sentence expresses a suggestion?

2 What type of verb are *should* and *must*?

▶▶ **Grammar Reference 4.2 p77**

PRACTICE

Suggestions and rules

1 Make suggestions. Use *I think/don't think … should.*

1 Peter's got the flu.
  I think he should go to bed. I don't think he should go to work.
2 I've lost my cheque book and credit cards.
3 Tony got his driving licence last week, and now he wants to drive from London to Edinburgh.
4 My teenage daughter doesn't get out of bed until noon.
5 I never have any money!
6 Jane and Paul are only 16, but they want to get married.
7 I'm really fed up with my job.
8 My grandparents complain they don't go out enough.

Do you have any problems? Ask the class for advice.

2 Write some rules for your school.

Students must arrive for lessons on time.

A new job

3 **T 4.7** Dave is about to start a new job. Listen to him talking to the manager. What's the job?

4 Work with a partner. Choose a job. Then ask and answer questions about the responsibilities, hours, breaks, etc.

Student A You are going to start the job next week.

Student B You are the boss.

What time do I have to start?

Do I have to wear a uniform?

When can I take a break?

Check it

5 Correct these sentences.

1 Do you can help me?
2 What time have you to start work?
3 We no allowed to wear jeans at school.
4 We no can do what we want.
5 My mother have to work very hard six days a week.
6 You no should smoke. It's bad for your health.
7 Passengers must to have a ticket.

WRITING: For and against
▶▶ Go to p60

READING AND SPEAKING
How to behave abroad

1 Are these statements true (✓) or false (✗) for people in your country?

1 ☐ When we meet someone for the first time, we shake hands.
2 ☐ Friends kiss on both cheeks when they meet or when they say goodbye.
3 ☐ We often invite people to our home for a meal.
4 ☐ If you have arranged to do something with friends, it's OK to be a little late.
5 ☐ You shouldn't yawn in public.
6 ☐ We call most people by their first names.

2 Read the text *A World Guide to Good Manners*. These lines have been taken out of the text. Where do they go?

a many people prefer not to discuss business while eating
b some businesses close in the early afternoon for a couple of hours
c for greeting, eating, or drinking
d the deeper you should bow
e should wear long-sleeved blouses and skirts below the knee

3 Answer the questions.
1 What nationality do you think the people in the pictures are?
2 What are the two differences between the American and the Japanese greeting?
3 List some of the clothes you think women *shouldn't* wear in Asian and Muslim countries.
4 Is your main meal of the day the same as in Italy or Spain?
5 In which countries do they prefer *not* to discuss business during meals?
6 What are some of the rules about business cards?
7 Why is it *not* a good idea to say to your Japanese business colleagues, 'I don't feel like staying out late tonight.'?
8 Which *Extra Tips* are about food and drink? Which ones are about general behaviour?

What do you think?

Discuss these questions in groups.

• There is a saying in English: 'When in Rome, do as the Romans do.' What does it mean? Do you agree? Do you have a similar saying in your language?

• Think of one or two examples of bad manners in your country. For example, in Britain it is considered impolite to ask people how much they earn.

• What advice would you give somebody coming to live and work in your country?

A WORLD GUIDE TO
Good Manners
How **not** to behave badly abroad

by Norman Ramshaw

Travelling to all corners of the world gets easier and easier. We live in a global village, but this doesn't mean that we all behave in the same way.

• Greetings

How should you behave when you meet someone for the first time? An American or Canadian shakes your hand firmly while looking you straight in the eyes. In many parts of Asia, there is no physical contact at all. In Japan, you should bow, and the more respect you want to show, (1)___. In Thailand, the greeting is made by pressing both hands together at the chest, as if you are praying, and bowing your head slightly. In both countries, eye contact is avoided as a sign of respect.

• Clothes

Many countries have rules about what you should and shouldn't wear. In Asian and Muslim countries, you shouldn't reveal the body, especially women, who (2)___.

In Japan, you should take off your shoes when entering a house or a restaurant. Remember to place them neatly together facing the door you came in. This is also true in China, Korea, Thailand, and Iran.

• Food and drink

In Italy, Spain, and Latin America, lunch is often the biggest meal of the day, and can last two or three hours. For this reason many people eat a light breakfast and a late dinner. In Britain, you might have a business lunch and do business as you eat. In Mexico and Japan, (3)___. Lunch is a time to relax and socialize, and the Japanese rarely drink alcohol at lunchtime. In Britain and the United States, it's not unusual to have a business meeting over breakfast, and in China it's common to have business banquets, but you shouldn't discuss business during the meal.

• Doing business

In most countries, an exchange of business cards is essential for all introductions. You should include your company name and your position. If you are going to a country where your language is not widely spoken, you can get the reverse side of your card printed in the local language. In Japan, you must present your card with both hands, with the writing facing the person you are giving it to.

In many countries, business hours are from 9.00 or 10.00 to 5.00 or 6.00. However in some countries, such as Greece, Italy, and Spain, (4)___ then remain open until the evening.

Japanese business people consider it their professional duty to go out after work with colleagues to restaurants, bars, or nightclubs. If you are invited, you shouldn't refuse, even if you don't feel like staying out late.

EXTRA TIPS

HERE ARE SOME EXTRA TIPS BEFORE YOU TRAVEL:

1 In many Asian cultures, it is acceptable to smack your lips when you eat. It means that the food is good.

2 In France, you shouldn't sit down in a café until you've shaken hands with everyone you know.

3 In India and the Middle East, you must never use the left hand (5)___.

4 In China, your host will keep refilling your dish unless you lay your chopsticks across your bowl.

5 Most South Americans and Mexicans like to stand very close to the person they're talking to. You shouldn't back away.

6 In Russia, you must match your hosts drink for drink or they will think you unfriendly.

7 In Ireland, social events sometimes end with singing and dancing. You may be asked to sing.

8 In America, you should eat your hamburger with both hands and as quickly as possible. You shouldn't try to have a conversation until it is eaten.

VOCABULARY
Nationality words

1 Match a line in **A** with a line in **B**. Notice the stress.

A	B
The I'talians	cook lots of noodles and rice.
The Chi'nese	wear kilts on special occasions.
The 'British	produce champagne.
The Ca'nadians	eat raw fish.
The French	invented football.
The Japa'nese	eat a lot of pasta.
The Scots	often watch ice hockey on TV.

T 4.8 Listen and check.

> **!**
> 1 All nationality words have capital letters in English.
>
> the French   the Italians   the British
>
> 2 If the adjective ends in /s/, /z/, /ʃ/, or /tʃ/ there is no *-s* at the end of the word for the people.
>
> Japanese   the Japanese
> Spanish   the Spanish
>
> 3 Sometimes the word for the people is different from the adjective.
>
> Scottish   the Scots
> Finnish   the Finns

2 Complete the chart and mark the stress. Add some more countries.

Country	Adjective	A sentence about the people
'Italy	I'talian	The Italians love pasta.
'Germany		
Aus'tralia		
'Scotland		
'Russia		
'Mexico		
the U'nited 'States		
'Greece		
'England		
'Sweden		

LISTENING AND SPEAKING
Come round to my place!

1 Have you ever been a guest in someone's home in a foreign country? When? Why? What was different?

2 **T 4.9** You will hear three people talking about inviting guests home for a meal. Listen and complete the chart.

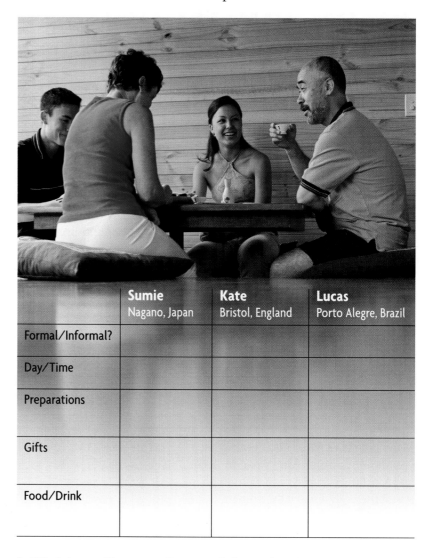

	Sumie Nagano, Japan	Kate Bristol, England	Lucas Porto Alegre, Brazil
Formal/Informal?			
Day/Time			
Preparations			
Gifts			
Food/Drink			

3 Work in small groups. Compare information.

4 What happens in your country? Is it usual to invite people to your home for a meal? What are such occasions like in your home?

EVERYDAY ENGLISH
Requests and offers

1 Match a line in **A** with a line in **B**. Who is talking? Where do you think the conversations are taking place?

A	B
1 Could you bring us the bill, please?	White or black?
2 Would you give me your work number, please?	No problem. It's stuffy in here.
3 Can I help you?	Of course. Oh, shall I give you my mobile number, too?
4 Two large coffees, please.	That line's engaged. Would you like to hold?
5 Can you tell me the code for Paris, please?	Yes, sir. I'll bring it right away.
6 I'll give you a lift if you like.	One moment. I'll look it up.
7 Would you mind opening the window?	Just looking, thanks.
8 Could I have extension 238, please?	That would be great! Could you drop me off at the library?

2 **T 4.10** Listen and check. Which are offers? Which are requests? Practise the conversations, paying particular attention to intonation and stress.

▶▶ **Grammar Reference 4.3 and 4.4 p78**

3 **T 4.11** Listen to the conversations. Complete the chart.

	Who are they?	**What are they talking about?**
1		
2		
3		
4		

T 4.11 Listen again. What are the words used to make the requests?

1 _____   3 _____

2 _____   4 _____

Roleplay

Work with a partner. Choose one of the situations and make up a conversation using the words.

Situation 1	Situation 2	Situation 3
Student A You are a customer in a restaurant. **Student B** You are a waiter/waitress.	**Student A** You are moving flat next week. **Student B** Offer to help.	**Student A** You are cooking a meal for 20 people. **Student B** Offer to help.
Use these words: • table near the window • menu • order • clean fork • dessert • bring the bill	**Use these words:** • pack boxes • load the van • clean • look after the plants • phone the gas board • unload the van	**Use these words:** • prepare the vegetables • make the salad • stir the sauce • check the meat • lay the table

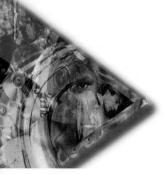

5 On the move

Future forms • The weather • Travelling around

TEST YOUR GRAMMAR

1 Match a sentence in **A** with a sentence in **B**. <u>Underline</u> the verb forms that refer to the future. What is the difference between them?

A	B
1 The phone's ringing.	I think it's going to rain.
2 Look at those black clouds!	Don't worry! It'll be spring soon.
3 What are you doing tonight?	We might go to Prague, or we might go to Budapest.
4 I'm sick and tired of winter!	I'll get it!
5 Where are you going on your holiday?	I'm staying at home. I'm going to watch a video.

I'll get it!

RING! RING!

2 Answer the questions about you.

• What are you doing after class today? • What's the weather forecast for tomorrow? • Where are you going on your next holiday?

BEN'S LIST
Future forms

1 Ben always writes a list at the beginning of the day. Read his list. Where's he going today? What's he going to do?

He's going to the hairdresser's.
He's going to buy some sugar.

Things to do
haircut
petrol
electricity bill — bank
tickets — travel agent
library
visit Nick?

Things to buy
sugar
yoghurt
milk
tennis balls

2 **T 5.1** Listen and complete the conversation between Ben and Alice.

B I'm going shopping. Do we need anything?

A I don't think so. … Oh, hang on. We haven't got any sugar.

B It's OK. It's on my list. I _____ some.

A What about bread?

B Good idea! I _____ a loaf.

A What time will you be back?

B I don't know. I might stop at Nick's. It depends on how much time I've got.

A Don't forget we _____ tennis with Dave and Donna this afternoon.

B Don't worry. I _____ forget. I _____ back before then.

A OK.

Memorize the conversation. Close your books and practise with a partner.

3 Alice also asks Ben to get these things.

- stamps
- two steaks
- some shampoo
- some film for the camera
- a newspaper
- a tin of white paint
- a video
- a CD

Which shops will Ben go to? Work with a partner to make conversations.

> *Can you get some stamps, please, honey?*

> *OK. I'll go to the post office.*

> *And we need some …
> Don't forget …*

GRAMMAR SPOT

1 Look at the future forms in these sentences from the conversation:

It's on my list. **I'm going to buy** some.
Good idea! **I'll get** a loaf.

In each sentence when did Ben make his decision? Before speaking, or at the moment of speaking?

2 Which of these sentences expresses a future possibility, which a prediction, and which a future arrangement?

We**'re playing** tennis this afternoon.
I **might stop** at Nick's.
I**'ll be** back before then.

▶▶ **Grammar Reference 5.1 p78**

PRACTICE

Discussing grammar

1 Work with a partner. <u>Underline</u> the correct verb form.

1 'Why are you putting on your coat?'
'Because *I'll take / I'm going to take* the dog for a walk.'

2 'Would you like to go out for a drink tonight?'
'How about tomorrow night? *I'll call / I'm calling* you.'

3 'What's the score?'
'6–0. *They're going to lose / They'll lose.*'

4 'It's Tony's birthday next week.'
'Is it? I didn't know. *I'll send / I'm going to send* him a card.'

5 'Are you and Alan still going out together?'
'Oh yes, *we'll get / we're getting* married in June.'

6 'Where are you going on holiday this year?'
'We haven't decided. *We might go / We're going to Italy.*'

What's going to happen?

2 **T 5.2** Listen to three short conversations. Say what is going to happen.

They're going to catch a plane.

What do you think will happen?

3 Make sentences using *I think ... will* and the prompts in **A**. Match them with a sentence in **B**.

I think Jerry will win the tennis match. He's been playing really well lately.

	A	B
1	Jerry/win the tennis match	But we'd better get going.
2	it/be a nice day tomorrow	He's been playing really well lately.
3	I/pass my exam on Friday	The forecast is for warm and dry weather.
4	you/like the film	You have the right qualifications and plenty of experience.
5	we/get to the airport in time	It's a wonderful story, and the acting is excellent.
6	you/get the job	I've been studying for weeks.

T 5.3 Listen and check. Practise saying them.

4 Make sentences using *I don't think ... will* and the prompts in **A** in exercise 3. Match them with a sentence in **C**.

I don't think Jerry will win the tennis match. He hasn't practised for weeks.

C
There's too much traffic.
I haven't studied at all.
The forecast said rainy and windy.
He hasn't practised for weeks.
They're looking for someone with more experience.
It's a bit boring.

T 5.4 Listen and check. Practise saying them.

Talking about you

5 Make true sentences about you starting with *I think ...* or *I don't think ... .*

1 I/bath tonight
2 the teacher/give us a lot of homework
3 I/eat out tonight
4 it/rain tomorrow
5 I/go shopping this afternoon
6 my partner/be a millionaire one day
7 we/have an exam this week

Arranging to meet

6 **T 5.5** Liz and Min Young are arranging to meet over the weekend. What plans do they already have? Listen and complete the chart. Where and what time do they arrange to meet?

Liz

	Liz	Min Young
FRIDAY		
morning		
afternoon		
evening		
SATURDAY		
morning		
afternoon		
evening		

Min Young

7 It is Friday morning. Fill in your diary for this weekend. What are you doing? When are you free?

Friday

morning

afternoon

evening

Saturday

morning

afternoon

evening

Sunday

morning

afternoon

evening

8 With a partner, think of a reason to get together this weekend. Arrange a day, time, and place to meet.

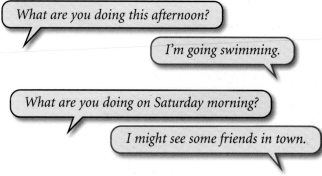

> *What are you doing this afternoon?*

> *I'm going swimming.*

> *What are you doing on Saturday morning?*

> *I might see some friends in town.*

When you have finished, tell the class when and where you're meeting.

We're meeting on Sunday morning at my flat. We're going to . . .

READING AND SPEAKING
Hotels with a difference

1 Look at the photos of the three hotels and answer these questions.
- Which countries do you think they are in?
- What do you think people can do on holiday there?

2 Write another question about each hotel.

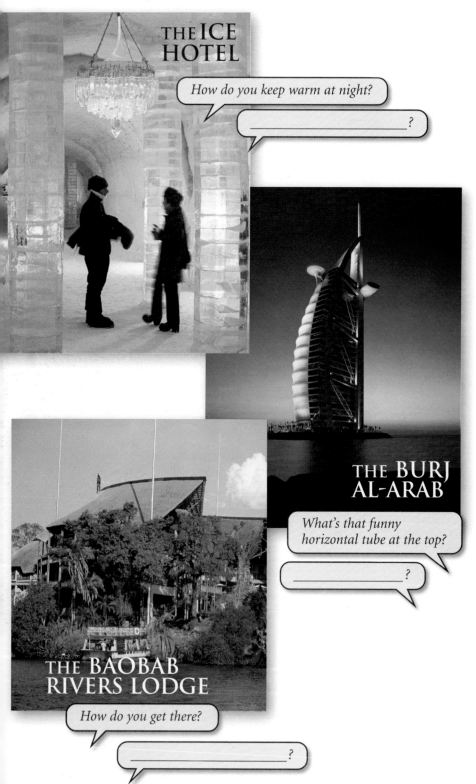

THE ICE HOTEL

How do you keep warm at night?

_____ ?

THE BURJ AL-ARAB

What's that funny horizontal tube at the top?

_____ ?

THE BAOBAB RIVERS LODGE

How do you get there?

_____ ?

3 Read the article and the brochure on p43. Which questions from exercise 2 can you answer? With a partner, answer these questions.
- What is Karen's job?
- Why does she take working holidays?
- What is her idea of a perfect holiday?
- Why does she spend her holidays at home?
- Animals are mentioned. Which ones, and why?

4 Complete the chart about Karen's trips to Canada and Dubai.

	Canada	Dubai
Which hotel is she staying at?		
How long is she staying there?		
What's special about the hotel and her room?		
What's she going to do there?		

5 Work with a partner. Look again at the brochure for the Baobab Rivers Lodge. Ask and answer questions about Karen's trip there.

Language work

Find words or expressions in the text with similar meanings.

My ideal holiday
1 doing nothing *lazing*
2 stopping to look around in
3 I'm very interested in
4 move around without any hurry

My business holidays
5 in an exciting and impressive way
6 things that should not be missed

What do you think?

- Do you know any unusual holiday destinations?
- In your opinion, what is *the* ideal holiday?
- Where are you going for your next holiday?

WRITING: Making a reservation
▶▶ Go to p61

My kind of **holiday**

She travels for her job, but when it's her own holiday, Karen Saunders stays at home.

Karen Saunders has her own travel agency in Mayfair, London that sends people all over the world on their dream holidays. She needs to know where she's sending them, so she goes on working holidays four or five times a year.

" My ideal holiday

My ideal holiday has a little bit of everything. I like lazing on a beach with a pile of books, but then I get bored and I need to do something. I love exploring new places, especially on foot, and nosing around in churches, shops, museums, and restaurants. I'm very into cooking, so I love going around markets and food stores.

However, I must confess that my favourite 'holiday resort' is home. I travel so much in my job that just waking up in my own bed is heaven. I potter around the house in my pyjamas, read the paper, do some gardening, shop for some food, then make a delicious meal in the evening.

My business holidays

I have three trips coming up. I'm looking forward to going to Canada soon, where I'm staying for four nights at the Ice Hotel. This is a giant igloo situated in Montmorency Fall Park, just 20 minutes from downtown Quebec. It is made from 4,500 tons of snow and 250 tons of ice, and it takes 5 weeks to build. It will stay open for three months. When the spring arrives, it will melt. Then it will be built again for next year – maybe in a different place! Each room is supplied with a sleeping bag made from deer skins. The hotel has two art galleries featuring ice sculptures, and an ice cinema. It also has a bar where all the drinks come in glasses made of ice. Of course I'll visit them all!

In complete contrast to the Ice Hotel, I'm going to Dubai the following month, to stay a few days at the spectacular Burj al-Arab, which means the Arabian Tower. It's shaped like a giant sail, and it rises dramatically out of the Arabian Gulf. Each room has sea views.

I really want to try the restaurant in the tube at the top next to the helipad. Other must-dos include shopping in the markets, called *souks*. (You can buy designer clothes, perfumes, and spices, but what I want is some gold jewellery.) I'm also going to visit the camel races.

The next trip, different again, is to Baobab Rivers, in Selous, Tanzania, for a seven-day safari and I'm looking forward to a few days...

THE BAOBAB RIVERS LODGE
IN SELOUS, TANZANIA

– so remote, you arrive by boat!

WHAT TO SEE Each tree-top room has views over the vast forested banks of the Rufiji River, which runs through one of the largest game reserves in Africa

WHAT TO DO Safari by Land Rover in search of elephants, rhinos, and lions; or by boat along the Rufiji River in search of crocodiles, hippos, and rare birds

LISTENING AND VOCABULARY
A weather forecast

1 Complete the chart with words from the box.

~~sunny~~	snowing			
windy	fog			
snowy	stormy			
ice	blowing			
wind	icy			
cloud	rain			
snow	cloudy			
shining	raining			
foggy	rainy			
sunshine				
(thunder)storm				

	Adjective	Noun	Verb
☀	It's _sunny._	_____	The sun's _____
🌧	It's _____	_____	It's _____
❄	It's _____	_____	It's _____
30→	It's _____	_____	The wind's _____

	Adjective	Noun
☁	It's _____	_____
⛈	It's _____	_____
FOG	It's _____	_____
ICE	It's _____	_____

2 Look at the map of Western Europe. Can you name the countries 1–10?

1 _____ 3 _____ 5 _____ 7 _____ 9 _____
2 _____ 4 _____ 6 _____ 8 _____ 10 _____

Which countries make up Scandinavia? Find them on the map.

In pairs, choose two of the countries and talk about:

- the climate
- the capital city
- geographical features

3 **T 5.6** Work in four groups A–D. Listen to the weather forecast and make notes about your part. When you have finished, swap information.

4 Work with a partner. What's the weather like where you are today? What do you think it will be like tomorrow? Write a forecast and read it to the class.

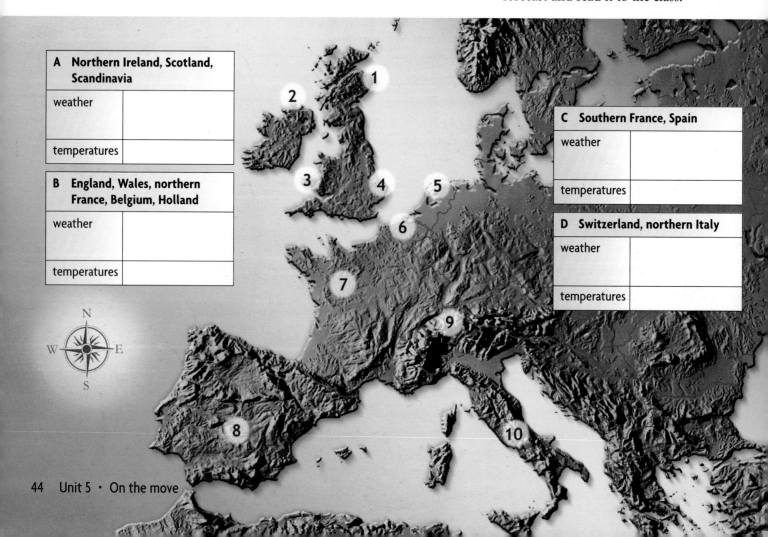

A Northern Ireland, Scotland, Scandinavia

weather	
temperatures	

B England, Wales, northern France, Belgium, Holland

weather	
temperatures	

C Southern France, Spain

weather	
temperatures	

D Switzerland, northern Italy

weather	
temperatures	

EVERYDAY ENGLISH
Travelling around

1 Here are some lines from conversations on different kinds of transport. Where does each conversation take place? Choose from the box.

> car bus taxi underground
> train plane ferry

1 Do you think it'll be a rough crossing?
2 Excuse me, I think those seats facing the front are ours.
3 We're going to Market Street. Could you tell us when it's our stop?
4 Can you take us to the airport?
5 Can I take these bags on with me?
6 That's all right. You can keep the change.
7 Excuse me, are we landing on time?
8 No, no! He said turn *left* at the lights, not right!
9 How do I get to Oxford Circus?

2 Match a line from exercise 1 with a reply.

a ☐ Look! *You* drive and *I'll* give directions from now on! Right?
b ☐ Of course. Hop in!
c ☐ I'm sorry. Only one item of hand luggage per passenger.
d ☐ Oh, I'm sorry. We didn't know they were reserved.
e ☐ Yes. We're beginning our descent soon.
f ☐ Well, the forecast is good, so it should be pretty smooth.
g ☐ Just sit near the front and I'll call it out.
h ☐ Take the Piccadilly Line, eastbound, and change at Green Park.
i ☐ Thanks a lot. Do you want a hand with those bags?

T 5.7 Listen and check. Practise the conversations with a partner.

Roleplay

Work with a partner. You are in a hotel.

Student A You are the receptionist.
Student B You are a guest.

The guest has several requests, and calls the front desk from his/her room. Use these situations. Change roles after three conversations.

- There are no towels in the room.
- You'd like some coffee and a sandwich in your room.
- You want the telephone number of the railway station.
- You want the front desk to recommend a good place to eat.
- You can't get the television to work.
- You want a wake-up call at 7.00 in the morning.
- You want to order a taxi to take you to the airport.

Can I help you?

Yes, there are no towels in my room. Could you send some up, please?

Certainly. I'll take care of it right away.

Thanks. Bye.

6 I just love it!

like · Verb patterns · Describing food, towns, and people · Signs and sounds

> *I look just like my dog.*

TEST YOUR GRAMMAR

1 Complete these sentences about you.

1 I look just like my . . .
2 I like my coffee . . .
3 On Sundays, I like . . .
4 After this class, I'd like to . . .
5 When I'm on holiday, I enjoy . . .
6 Yesterday evening, I decided to . . .

2 Tell the class some of the things you wrote.

A STUDENT VISITOR
Questions with *like*

1 Many students go to study in a foreign country. Do you know anyone who has studied abroad?

2 Sandy and her friend Nina in Melbourne, Australia, are talking about a student visitor from South Korea. Complete the conversation using these questions.

What does she like doing?	How is she now?	What's she like?
What does she look like?	What would she like to do?	

Sandy Our student from Seoul arrived on Monday.
Nina What's her name?
Sandy Soon-hee.
Nina That's a pretty name!
(1) _____
Sandy She's really nice. I'm sure we'll get on well. We seem to have a lot in common.
Nina How do you know that already?
(2) _____
Sandy Well, she likes dancing, and so do I. And we both like listening to the same kind of music.
Nina (3) _____
Sandy Oh, she's really pretty. She has big, brown eyes and long, dark hair.

Nina Why don't we do something with Soon-hee this weekend? What should we do? Get a pizza? Go clubbing? (4) _____
Sandy I'll ask her tonight. She was a bit homesick at first, so I'm pretty sure she'll want to go out and make some friends.
Nina (5) _____
Sandy Oh, she's OK. She called her parents and she felt much better after she'd spoken to them.
Nina Oh, that's good. I can't wait to meet her.

T 6.1 Listen and check. Practise the conversation with a partner.

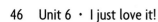

GRAMMAR SPOT

1 Write a question from exercise 2 next to the correct definition.

Question	Definition
a _____	= Tell me about her because I don't know anything about her.
b _____	= Tell me about her physical appearance.
c _____	= Tell me about her interests and hobbies.
d _____	= Tell me about her preferences for tomorrow evening.
e _____	= Tell me about her health or happiness.

2 Which questions use *like* as a verb? Which questions use *like* as a preposition?

▶▶ **Grammar Reference 6.1–6.3 pp79–80**

PRACTICE

Talking about you

1 Ask and answer with a partner.

- What do you like doing at the weekend?
- Who do you look like in your family?
- How are your parents and grandparents?
- What is your best friend like?
- What's your school like?
- What does your teacher look like?

Listening and asking questions

2 **T 6.2** Listen and tick (✓) the question each person is answering.

1. ☐ Do you like Thai food?
   ☐ What's Thai food like?

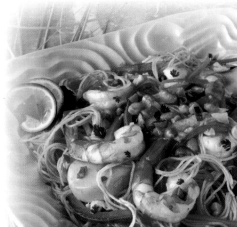

2. ☐ Who does Bridget look like?
   ☐ What's Bridget like?
3. ☐ How's your brother?
   ☐ What's your brother like?
4. ☐ What does she like?
   ☐ What does she look like?
5. ☐ What's the weather like there?
   ☐ Do you like the weather there?
6. ☐ What does he look like?
   ☐ What's he like?
7. ☑ What do you like doing on holiday?
   ☑ What was your holiday like?
8. ☒ What kind of books do you like?
   ☐ What kind of books would you like?

A THANK-YOU LETTER
Verb patterns

Soon-hee has returned home to Seoul. Read her letter and choose the correct verb form.

SOON-HEE

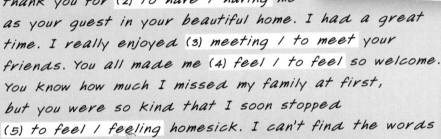

Sang-chul and me

Seoul
December 15

Dear Sandy and family,
   I just wanted (1) (to say) / saying
thank you for (2) to have / having me
as your guest in your beautiful home. I had a great
time. I really enjoyed (3) meeting / to meet your
friends. You all made me (4) feel / to feel so welcome.
You know how much I missed my family at first,
but you were so kind that I soon stopped
(5) to feel / feeling homesick. I can't find the words
to tell you how grateful I am. I'd like
(6) to call / calling you. What's a good time to call?
   You know that on my way home I stopped
(7) to visit / visiting my aunt in Perth. It was
so hot! It was over 35 degrees all the time
but I absolutely loved it. My aunt wanted
(8) that I stay / me to stay longer, but I wanted
(9) to see / seeing my parents and my brother, Sang-chul.
But she's invited me (10) to go / going back and I'd love
(11) to do / to doing that. I'm thinking of (12) go / going
next year.
   Anyway, I'm looking forward to (13) hear / hearing from
you very soon. Let me (14) to know / know if you ever want
to visit Seoul. My brother and I could take you to a
'norebang' (a singing room). It's a bit like karaoke!
Love to you all,

   Soon-hee

p.s. Do you like the picture of Sang-chul and me?

RSON
A DRIVE
URNE 8100
RALIA

T 6.3 Listen and check.

Verb patterns

1 Complete these examples from Soon-hee's letter.
   a I really **enjoyed** _____ your friends.
   b I just **wanted** _____ _____ thank you.
   c My aunt **wanted** _____ _____ _____ longer.
   d You all **made** _____ _____ so welcome.
   e **Thank you** _____ _____ me as your guest.

2 Match a sentence with a picture.
   1 They **stopped to talk** to each other.
   2 They **stopped talking** to each other.

What's the difference in meaning between sentences 1 and 2?

3 Complete these examples from the letter.
   I soon stopped _____ homesick.
   I stopped _____ my aunt.

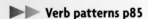 **Verb patterns p85**

PRACTICE

What's the pattern?

1 Write the examples from Soon-hee's letter on the chart.

verb + -ing	verb + to + infinitive	verb + sb + to + infinitive	verb + sb + infinitive (no to)	preposition + -ing
enjoyed meeting				

2 **T 6.4** Listen to the sentences. Write each verb in the correct column in exercise 1.

promise   succeed in   **let**

tell   **ask**   help

finish   need   **hate**

forget   don't mind   look forward to

Check your answers on p85.

Discussing grammar

3 In these sentences, two verbs are correct and one is not. Tick (✓) the correct verbs.
   1 My father _____ to mend my bike.
      a ☑ promised   b ☐ couldn't   c ☑ tried
   2 She _____ her son to turn down his music.
      a ☐ asked   b ☐ wanted   c ☐ made
   3 I _____ going on long walks.
      a ☐ refuse   b ☐ can't stand   c ☐ love
   4 We _____ to go shopping.
      a ☐ need   b ☐ 'd love   c ☐ enjoy
   5 She _____ me do the cooking.
      a ☐ wanted   b ☐ made   c ☐ helped
   6 I _____ working for the bank 20 years ago.
      a ☐ started   b ☐ stopped   c ☐ decided

4 Make correct sentences using the other verbs in exercise 3.
   My father couldn't mend my bike.

READING AND SPEAKING
The world's favourite food

NAPLES, ITALY, ON VALENTINE'S DAY

1 Do you know any typical dishes from these countries? Discuss with the class.

• Spain	• Japan	• Mexico
• Italy	• Hungary	• the United States
• Germany	• China	• England

Can you think of any foods that might be popular in all of the countries above?

2 Which of these are fish or seafood?

> oil garlic anchovies eel squid herring salmon
> peas shrimp pineapple bacon tuna sweetcorn

T 6.5 Listen and repeat.

3 Work in groups. Read the text quickly and find the foods in exercise 2. How many other foods can you find?

4 Read the text again and answer the questions.
  1 What does *McDonald's Golden Arches span the globe* mean?
  2 What are the similarities and differences between the hamburger and the pizza?
  3 What year was pizza invented?
  4 Which came first, *picea* or *plakuntos*? How are they different from pizza?
  5 Why are Mexico and Peru important in the development of pizza?
  6 What do the Italian flag and a Pizza Margherita have in common?
  7 When and how did pizza become really popular in the United States?

PIZZA IN SPACE

5 Work in groups. Read *Pizza Trivia* again and make questions.

How many . . . ?	How much . . . ?	Which month . . . ?
Where and when . . . ?	Which toppings . . . ?	

Close your books. Ask and answer questions.

What do you think?

• Which facts in Pizza Trivia do you find most interesting? Why?
• Why do different countries prefer such different toppings?
• Do you like pizza? What are your favourite toppings?
• What are the most popular places to eat in your country? Why?
• What is your favourite place to eat?

Language work

Study the text and find an example of:

• *like* used as a verb
• *like* used as a preposition
• verb + *-ing* form
• verb + infinitive
• adjective + infinitive

GL⬤BAL PIZZA

BY CONNIE ODONE

So you thought the hamburger was the world's most popular fast food? After all, McDonald's Golden Arches span the globe. But no, there is another truly universal fast food, the ultimate fast food. It's easy to make, easy to serve, much more varied than the hamburger, can be eaten with the hands, and it's delivered to your front door or served in fancy restaurants. It's been one of America's favourite foods for over 50 years. It is, of course, the pizza.

A BRIEF HISTORY OF PIZZA

It's kind of silly to talk about the moment when pizza was 'invented'. It gradually evolved over the years, but one thing's for certain – it's been around for a very long time. The idea of using pieces of flat, round bread as plates came from the Greeks. They called them 'plakuntos' and ate them with various simple toppings such as oil, garlic, onions, and herbs. The Romans enjoyed eating something similar and called it 'picea'. By about 1000 a.d. in the city of Naples, 'picea' had become 'pizza' and people were experimenting with more toppings: cheese, ham, anchovies, and finally the tomato, brought to Italy from Mexico and Peru in the sixteenth century. Naples became the pizza capital of the world. In 1889, King Umberto I and Queen Margherita heard about pizza and asked to try it. They invited pizza maker, Raffaele Esposito, to make it for them. He decided to make the pizza like the Italian flag, so he used red tomatoes, white mozzarella cheese, and green basil leaves. The Queen loved it and the new pizza was named 'Pizza Margherita' in her honour.

Pizza migrated to America with the Italians at the end of the nineteenth century. The first pizzeria in the United States was opened in 1905 at 53½ Spring Street, New York City, by Gennaro Lombardi. But the popularity of pizza really exploded when American soldiers returned from Italy after World War II and raved about 'that great Italian dish'. Americans are now the greatest producers and consumers of pizza in the world.

PIZZA TRIVIA

1 Americans eat 350 slices of pizza per second.
2 There are 61,269 pizzerias in the United States.
3 Pizza is a $30 billion per year industry.
4 October is national pizza month in the United States.
5 The world's first pizzeria, the Antica Pizzeria Port'Alba, which opened in Naples in 1830, is still there.
6 Pizza Hut has over 12,000 restaurants and takeaway outlets in over 90 countries.
7 In America, pepperoni is the favourite topping. Anchovies is the least favourite.
8 In Japan, eel and squid are favourites. In Russia it's red herring, salmon and onions.
9 In Brazil, they like green peas on their pizza. In Australia the favourites are shrimp and pineapple.
10 The French love bacon and crème fraîche on theirs. The English love tuna and sweetcorn.

VOCABULARY
Adjectives for food, towns, and people

1 In each group, *four* of the adjectives cannot go with the noun. Which ones?

junk fast **delicious** tasteless
fresh
disgusting **FOOD** plain tasteful
~~disgusted~~ vegetarian
frozen home-grown wealthy starving
rich

excited home old university
exciting young
polluted **TOWN** modern
capital busy
industrial agricultural
antique cosmopolitan historic small

young sophisticated long elderly antique
expensive **PEOPLE** shy starving
bored boring rude
wealthy sociable outgoing crowded tall

2 Complete the conversations with adjectives from exercise 1. Where necessary, use the comparative or superlative forms.

1 **A** Nick's really quiet and _____. He never says a word.
  B Yeah, his brother is much _____ _____.

2 **A** What's Carrie's boyfriend like?
  B Well, he's _____, dark, and handsome, but he's not very polite. In fact, he's even _____ than Carrie!

3 **A** How was your lunch?
  B Ugh! It was awful. The pizza was _____. We were really _____, but we still couldn't eat it!

4 **A** Mmm! These tomatoes are really _____. Did you grow them yourselves?
  B Yes, we did. All our vegetables are _____.

5 **A** Did you have a good time in London?
  B We had a great time. There's so much to do. It's a really _____ city. And there are so many people from all over the world. I think it's nearly as _____ as New York.

T 6.6 Listen and check. Practise the conversations with a partner.

Talking about you

3 Work with a partner. Look at p83.

LISTENING AND SPEAKING
New York and London

1 Look at the pictures of New York and London. Write down what you know about these cities. Compare your lists as a class. Has anyone been to either city?

2 Work in two groups.

Group A **T 6.7** Listen to Justin and Cinda who are English but live and work in New York.

Group B **T 6.8** Listen to Alan, an American, who lives and works in London.

What do they say about these things?

• people • work/holidays • shops
• places • getting around • food

3 Find a partner from the other group. Compare your information.

EVERYDAY ENGLISH
Signs and sounds

1 Where would you see these things written?

1 All visitors must sign in

5 Coats and other articles left at owner's risk.

6 PLEASE WAIT TO BE SEATED

2  100% NYLON
DRY CLEAN ONLY
COOL IRON
DO NOT IRON TRIM
MADE IN INDIA

7 IRRITANT
CONTAINS SODIUM HYPOCHLORITE
Keep out of reach of children –
do not mix with other laundry cleaners.
contact with acid liberates toxic gas. Irritating to eyes and skin.
Avoid contact with eyes.
In case of contact with eyes, rinse immediately with plenty of water

3 Pay and Display

8 LIGHTS
SMOKING CAUSES
FATAL DISEASES

4  Also contains: White Soft Paraffin
Purified Water.

FOR EXTERNAL USE ONLY

Do not use after the expiry date sh
CROOKES   Crookes Hea

9  Arrivals →
Baggage reclaim

10 **!** KEEP CLEAR

2 Where would you hear these things?

> Coming up next – traffic, news, and the weather.

> Please listen carefully to the following options. To purchase tickets for today's performance, press one . . .

> Please place your tray tables in their fully upright and locked positions.

> How would you like the money?

> Just looking, thanks.

> We apologize for the delay on the 18.13 service.

WRITING: A description (1)
▶▶ Go to p62

BLANK PAGE

Writing

UNIT 1 *p13*

CORRECTING MISTAKES (1)

1 It is important to try to correct your own mistakes when you write. Look at the letter that a student has written to her friend. Her teacher has used symbols to show her the kind of mistakes she has made. Read the letter and correct the mistakes.

T Tense	WW Wrong word
Prep Preposition	P Punctuation
Gr Grammar	Sp Spelling
WO Word order	⋏ Word missing

23, St. Mary's Road,
Dublin 4, Ireland
Tuesday, 10 May

Dear Stephanie

How are you? I'm very well. I came <u>in</u> [Prep] Dublin two weeks ago <u>for to</u> [Gr] study at a language school. I want⋏learn <u>e</u>nglish [P] because⋏is a very important language. I'm <u>stay</u> [Gr] with <u>a</u> [Gr] Irish family. They've got two <u>son</u> [Gr] and a daughter. Mr Kendall is⋏teacher and Mrs Kendall <u>work</u> [Gr] in a hospital. The Irish <u>is</u> [Gr] very kind, but they speak very quickly!

I study in the morning. My teacher<u>s</u> [P] name is Ann. She <u>said</u> [WW] me that my English is OK, but I <u>do</u> [WW] a lot of mistakes. Ann <u>don't</u> [Gr] give us too much homework, so in the afternoons I <u>go always</u> [WO] sightseeing. Dublin is much <u>more big</u> [Gr] than my town. I like <u>very much painting</u> [WO] and I'm very interest<u>ing</u> [Gr] <u>for</u> [Prep] modern art, so I visit galleries and museums. I've met a girl named Martina. She <u>came</u> [T] from Spain and <u>go</u> [Gr] to Trinity College. Last night we <u>go</u> [T] to the cinema, but the film wasn't very <u>exiting</u> [Sp].

<u>Do</u> [WW] you like to visit me? Why don't you come for a weekend?

I'd love to see you.

Write to me soon.

Love, *Kati*

2 Answer the questions.
1 Where is Kati? Where is she staying?
2 Why is she there?
3 What does she do each day?
4 What does she do in her free time?
5 Who has she met?

3 Imagine that you are a student in another town. Answer the questions in exercise 2 about *you*.

4 Write a similar letter to a friend back in your country. Write 150–200 words.

LETTERS AND EMAILS
Beginnings and endings

1 How many different ways can you think of to start and end a letter or email?

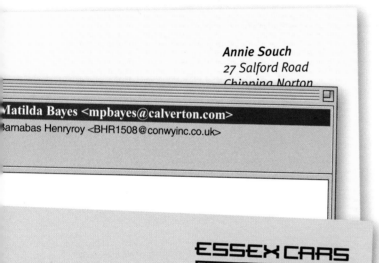

wishes   madam   All   Hi!   sir
Dear   Lots of   love   best
sincerely   Yours   faithfully

2 Read extracts 1–11 from some letters and emails. Which are beginnings and which are endings? Write **B** or **E**.

1 <u>Just a note</u> to say thank you so much for having me to stay last weekend. **B**

2 Thank you for your letter of 16 April. Please find enclosed a cheque for £50.00.

3 Write or better still, email me soon.

4 How are you doing? You'll never guess who I saw last week at Dan's.

5 I am writing in response to your advertisement in yesterday's *Daily Star*.

6 We trust this arrangement meets with your satisfaction.

7 I'm sorry I haven't been in touch for such a long time.

8 I look forward to hearing from you at your earliest convenience.

9 I thought I'd write rather than email for a change.

10 Give my regards to Robert.

11 Take care and thanks again.

3 Look again at the sentences in exercise 2. Which are formal, and which are informal? <u>Underline</u> the words and phrases which helped you decide.

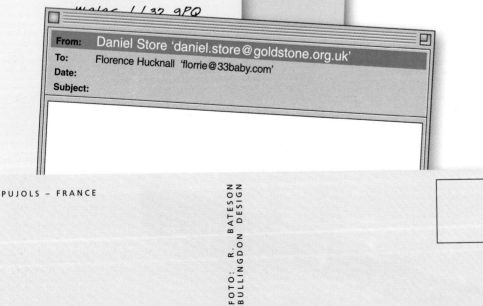

4 Match the beginnings and endings of these different letters and emails.

Beginnings	Endings
1 Dear Mary and Dave, Any chance that you two are free next Sat. p.m.?	• Many thanks. I look forward to hearing from you in the near future. Yours faithfully, James Fox
2 Dear Jane, Thanks for your letter. It was great to hear from you after such a long time. You asked me what I've been doing. Well, . . .	• We apologize for the inconvenience and will have pleasure in processing your order as soon as we receive the additional amount. Yours sincerely, Thames Valley Computer Software
3 Dear Sir/Madam, I saw an advertisement in the *Daily Telegraph* for weekend breaks at your hotel.	• It would be lovely to see you some time. Do you ever come to London? We could meet for lunch. Love Pat
4 Hi Pete, Thanks for the invite.	• Let me know asap. All the best, Martin
5 Dear Mr Smith, We received your order for the Encyclopedia World CD ROM, and your cheque for £75.	• Can't wait to see you. Let's hope it stays fine. Love to Ellie. See you then. Deborah

5 Continue the beginnings with one of these lines.

☐ Could you please send me your brochure and a price list? I would be most grateful.

☐ I've changed my job a few times since I last spoke to you, and as you know, I've moved to a new flat.

☐ Unfortunately, this amount did not include packing and postage, which is £7.50.

☐ We've got four tickets for that open-air concert in Woodstock. Interested?

☐ We'd love to come.

6 Which one . . .

- asks for information?
- invites?
- asks for further payment?
- accepts an invitation?
- gives news?

<u>Underline</u> the words and phrases which helped you decide.

7 You have just found the email address of an old friend on the website *Friends Reunited*. Write an email to him/her. Give your news, describe some things that you have done recently, and say what your future plans are. Ask about his/her news and family.

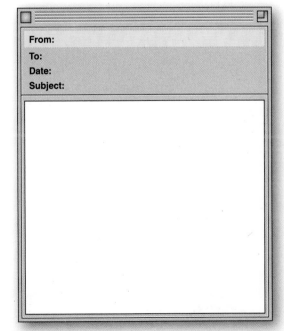

From:
To:
Date:
Subject:

A NARRATIVE (1)
Telling a story – linking ideas

1 Read the story. Where do clauses a–f go?

   a as soon as their father had died
   b who had worked hard in his vineyard
      all his life
   c what their father had meant by the
      great treasure
   d and while they were working they
      thought about what their father had
      said
   e because they felt that all their hard
      work had been for nothing
   f Soon they had dug up every inch of
      the vineyard

   Complete the moral.

THE FARMER AND HIS SONS

There was once an old, dying farmer (1)___. Before he died he wanted
to teach his three sons how to be good farmers. So he called them to his
bedside and said, 'My boys, I have an important secret to tell you: there
is a great treasure buried in the vineyard. Promise me that you will look
for it when I am dead.'

   The sons gave their promise and (2)___ they began looking for the
treasure. They worked very hard in the hot sun (3)___. They pictured
boxes of gold coins, diamond necklaces, and other such things. (4)___
but they found not a single penny. They were very upset (5)___.
However, a few months later the grapes started to appear on the vines.
Their grapes were the biggest and best in the neighbourhood and they
sold them for a lot of money. Now the sons understood (6)___ and they
lived happily ever after.

THE MORAL OF THIS STORY IS: HARD WORK BRINGS . . .

2 Complete the sentences using a linking word from the box. Use each linking word once only.

THE EMPEROR AND HIS DAUGHTERS

There was once an emperor _____ lived in a palace.
He had three daughters _____ no sons.
He wanted his daughters to marry _____ he died.
He found three princes. _____ his daughters didn't like them.
They refused to marry the princes, _____ the emperor became very angry.
He said they must get married _____ they were sixteen years old.
The three daughters ran away _____ the night and found work on a farm.
They fell in love with the farmer's sons _____ they were working there.
They married the sons _____ they were sixteen.

| before |
| as soon as |
| while |
| during |
| when |
| but |
| However, |
| so |
| who |

3 In what ways are these sentences different from the ones in exercise 2?

There was once an old emperor who lived in an enormous, golden palace in the middle of the city Ping Chong. He had three beautiful daughters, but unfortunately no sons.

Continue rewriting the story, adding more detail to make it more interesting.

4 Write a folk tale or fairy story that you know. Write about 200 words.

Begin:

There was/were once ...

or

Once upon a time there was/were ...

End:

... and they lived happily ever after.

If your story has a moral, give it at the end.

FOR AND AGAINST

1 Read the text. Replace the underlined words and phrases with those in the box.

in my opinion,	One advantage is that	For instance
One disadvantage is that	pros and cons	All things considered
Finally	In conclusion	In fact,
Another point is that	Moreover	

CHILDHOOD
– the best time of your life

1 Some people say that childhood is the best time of your life. However, being a child has both <u>advantages and disadvantages</u>.

2 <u>On the plus side,</u> you have very few responsibilities. <u>For example,</u> you don't have to go to work, pay bills, or do the shopping, cooking, or cleaning. This means you have plenty of free time to do whatever you want – watch TV; play on the computer; go out with friends; play sports, or pursue other hobbies. <u>On top of that</u>, public transport, cinema, and sports centres cost much less for children. <u>All in all</u>, being a child is an exciting, action-packed time in life.

3 However, for every plus there is a minus. <u>For one thing,</u> you have to spend all day, Monday to Friday, at school. Studying usually means you have to do homework, and you have to take exams. <u>What is more</u>, you may have a lot of free time, but you are rarely allowed to do whatever you want. You usually have to ask your parents if you can do things, from going shopping in town to staying out late or going to a party. <u>Last of all</u>, although there are often cheaper prices for children, things are still expensive – and parents are not always generous with pocket money. There's never enough to do everything you want. <u>The reality is that</u> sometimes there's not enough to do anything at all!

4 <u>To sum up</u>, although some people see childhood as the best time in life, <u>I think that</u> children have no real choice, independence, or money. Nevertheless, it is true that choice, money, and independence all bring responsibilities and restrictions – which increase with age.

2 There are four paragraphs. What is the purpose of each one?

3 Match the pros with the cons.

	Pros	Cons
1	don't have to go to work	are never given enough pocket money
2	can go out to parties with friends	have to do homework and take exams
3	don't have to cook and clean	have to go to school Monday to Friday
4	costs less to do things	need to ask your parents' permission

4 You are going to write a 'for and against' essay. Write a list of pros and cons for one of these topics.

1 Getting older
2 Having a university degree
3 Having children while young

5 Use your ideas from exercise 4 to write four paragraphs. Write about 250 words.

MAKING A RESERVATION

1 Janet Cooper wants to go on holiday with her family. She faxes the Sea View B&B to see if they have the accommodation she wants. Look at the advert for the Sea View B&B and fill in the details at the top of the fax.

2 Put the words in order, and write them into the message part of Janet's fax.

SEA VIEW B&B
www.seaviewb&b.com

Get away from the city.
Escape to the peace and quiet
of Cornwall!

For reservations and enquiries contact
Anne Westcombe:
  Phone/Fax: 01326 230579
  email: reservations@seaviewb&b.com

FAX TRANSMISSION

To: _____

From: Janet Cooper

Subject: _____

Page 1 of 1

Date: _____

To fax no.: _____

From fax no.: 01259 67821

---

a two / rooms / bed and breakfast / I / to / would like / reserve / at / your

b 27 August / We / on / are / arriving

c six / hope / stay / to / We / for / nights / departing / 2 September / on

d and / husband / would like / room / I / My / double / with / en-suite bathroom / an / preferably / a

e also / reserve / two / to / I / a / room / for / would / like / teenage / our / daughters

f should / non-smoking / rooms / be / Both

g sea / the / possible / Would / have / it / rooms / to / facing / be / ?

h available / for / you / Do / have / dates / these / rooms / ?

i also / me / you / Could / tell / room / each / price / the / of / ?

j from / I / forward / look / you / to / hearing

3 Write a reply letter or fax to Janet. Include the following information:

- thank her for her enquiry
- say you are pleased to confirm her reservation for the rooms she wants and for the dates she wants
- tell her that all the rooms come with en-suite bathroom and a sea view
- each room is £50 per night
- end the letter saying that you look forward to welcoming her and her family to the B&B
- finish with **Yours sincerely, Anne Westcombe**

A DESCRIPTION (1)
Describing a room – relative pronouns, participles

1 Think of your favourite room. Draw a plan of it on a piece of paper. Write down why you like it and some adjectives to describe it.

My favourite room is . . .   I like it because . . .

Show a partner your plan and talk about your room.

2 Read the description. Why is this kitchen more than just a room where you cook and eat?

3 Complete the description using these relative clauses:

> which tells the story
> that we're going to next Saturday
> where we cook and eat
> whose family have all emigrated
> which is the focal point of the room
> which means
> we haven't seen
> I like best
> who are cross and sleepy
> where family and friends come together

GRAMMAR SPOT

1 Underline the relative pronouns in exercise 3. What do they refer to? When do we use *which, who, that, where,* and *whose*?

2 Look at the these sentences. We can omit the relative pronoun from one in each pair. Which one? Why?

This is the room **which** I like best. / This is the room **which** has a good view of the sea.

He's a friend **who** we haven't seen for years. / He's a friend **who** lives in London.

3 Look at these examples of participles. Rewrite them with relative pronouns.

I have so many happy memories of times **spent** there.

There is a large window **looking** out onto two apple trees in the garden.

▶▶ **Grammar Reference 6.5 and 6.6 p80**

My favourite room

The room in our house (1)_____ is our kitchen. Perhaps the kitchen is the most important room in many houses, but it is particularly so in our house because it's not only (2)_____, but it's also the place (3)_____.

I have so many happy memories of times spent there: ordinary daily events such as making breakfast on dark, cold winter mornings for children (4)_____, before sending them off to school; or special occasions such as homecomings or cooking Christmas dinner. Whenever we have a party, people gravitate with their drinks to the kitchen. It always ends up the fullest and noisiest room in the house.

So what does this special room look like? It's quite big, but not huge. It's big enough to have a good-sized rectangular table in the centre, (5)_____. There is a large window above the sink, looking

out onto two apple trees in the garden. There's a big, old cooking stove at one end, and at the other end a wall with a huge notice board (6)_____ of our lives, past, present, and future: a school photo of the kids; a postcard from Auntie Nancy, (7)_____ to Australia; the menu from a take-away Chinese restaurant; an invitation to a wedding (8)_____; a letter from a friend (9)_____ for years. All our world is there for everyone to read!

The front door is seldom used in our house, only by strangers. All our friends use the back door (10)_____ they come straight into the kitchen and join in whatever is happening there. The kettle goes on immediately and then we all sit round the table, drinking tea and putting the world to rights! Without doubt some of the happiest times of my life have been spent in our kitchen.

4 Link these sentences with the correct relative pronoun: *who, which, that, where, whose.*

1 The blonde lady is Pat. She's wearing a black dress.
2 There's the hospital. My sister works there.
3 The postcard arrived this morning. It's from Auntie Nancy.
4 I passed all my exams. This made my father very proud.
5 Did you meet the girl? Her mother teaches French.

5 Complete the sentences with a word from the box in the present or past participle.

| play give stick listen arrange |

1 I spend hours in my room, _____ to music.
2 I have lots of posters _____ on the walls.
3 My brother is in his bedroom, _____ on his computer.
4 There are photos of my family _____ on my shelves.
5 I also have a colour TV _____ to me on my last birthday.

6 Write a similar description of your favourite room in about 250 words. Describe it and give reasons why you like it. Use relative pronouns and participles to link your sentences.

Tapescripts

Unit 1

T 1.1 **General knowledge quiz**

1 The modern Olympic Games started in 1896.
2 It takes eight minutes for the sun's rays to reach the Earth.
3 He was walking on the moon.
4 If you are flying over the International Date Line, the Pacific Ocean is below you.
5 A vegetarian doesn't eat meat.
6 www. stands for World Wide Web.
7 Glasses were invented in Italy around 1300 A.D.
8 Brazil has won the World Cup five times.
9 John Lennon was returning to his apartment when he was assassinated.
10 Chinese is spoken by the most people in the world.
11 Nelson Mandela didn't become president of South Africa until he was 76 years old because he was in prison for 27 years.
12 People have been sending emails since the 1970s.

T 1.2

1 The sun doesn't rise in the west! It rises in the east!
2 Cows don't eat meat! They eat grass!
3 Mercedes-Benz cars aren't made in Canada! They're made in Germany!
4 Neil Armstrong didn't land on the moon in 1989! He landed in 1969!
5 John Lennon wasn't performing on stage when he was assassinated! He was returning to his apartment!
6 The Pyramids weren't built by the Chinese! They were built by the Egyptians!
7 We haven't been in class for five hours! We've been in class for one hour!
8 We aren't studying Italian! We're studying English!

T 1.3

1 A What did you do last night?
  B I stayed at home and watched television.
2 A What kind of books do you like reading?
  B Horror stories and science fiction.
3 A Have you ever been to the United States?
  B Yes, I have. I went there last year.
  A Did you like it?
  B Yes, I really enjoyed it.
4 A What's the teacher doing?
  B He's helping Maria with this exercise.
5 A What does your mother do?
  B She works in a bank.
6 A Why didn't you do your homework last night?
  B Because I didn't feel well.
7 A What are you doing next weekend?
  B I'm going to a party.
8 A Have you got a TV in your bedroom?
  B No, I haven't. Just a CD player.

T 1.4

1 My sister's a teacher.
2 She's on holiday at the moment.

3 She's in France.
4 She's never travelled to Europe before.
5 She's been there for two weeks.
6 She's going back to work next week.
7 Her husband's a builder.
8 He's got his own business.

T 1.5 **See p8**

T 1.6 **Making conversation**

D = Dad, E = Emma

D Good morning! Did you have a nice time last night?
E Yes, I did. I went round to Bill's house.
D Do you want breakfast?
E No, I don't, thanks. I'm not hungry.
D Have you had any coffee?
E Yes, I have. I don't want any more, thanks.
D Is Bill coming round tonight?
E No, he isn't. He's going out for dinner with his family.
D OK. Are you leaving for school soon?
E Yes, I am. I'm going right now. Bye!

T 1.7

1 Is it hot today?
2 Is it raining?
3 Are you wearing trainers?
4 Do you usually come to class by bus?
5 Are you going out tonight?
6 Did you have a good day yesterday?
7 Have you got a dictionary?
8 Have you got any pets?

T 1.8

1 A Do you like studying English?
  B Yes, I do. It's my favourite subject.
2 A Is it a nice day today?
  B No, it isn't. It's freezing.
3 A Have you seen my pen?
  B No, I haven't. You can borrow mine if you want.
4 A Are you staying at home this evening?
  B Yes, I am. Do you want to come round?
5 A Did you go on holiday last summer?
  B No, I didn't. I couldn't afford to.

T 1.9 **My wonders**

K = Kelly, S = Sam, P = Peter

K We were doing the wonders of the world in school today. You know, the seven ancient wonders, the pyramids and such like and we got to talking about what modern wonders would be and well we all thought that …
S Huh! I know what the best modern wonder is for me. I know what's changed *my* life more than anything else …
P What's that, Dad?
S The dishwasher.
K Uh? What d'you mean – the dishwasher?
S I mean the dishwasher. I think it's marvellous! Every time I use something – cups, plates, dishes, knives, forks, you know, I just put it in, and after a few days it fills up, I turn it on and 'bingo' – all clean, bright and sparkling and I start again. Helps keep my kitchen tidy. I'm not very good at tidyi …

K Yeah, and the rest of the house is a mess! Come on Grandpa, be a bit more serious, we …
S I *am* serious!
K Well, anyway, *we* all said at school the very best thing was the mobile phone …
P I knew it!
S Huh! I don't even know how to use one.
K Oh, I couldn't live without mine. It's brilliant. I can call or text my friends all the time …
P Don't I know …
K … from wherever I am and they can call or text me. Or if I need a lift from you or Mum …
P You mean like when you need picking up from a friend's house in the evening?
K Yeah, that kind of thing … or if I'm going to be home late, or like staying late at school or whatever – I can just let you and Mum know what's happening.
S OK, OK that's good, but the problem is that people use them too much for every little thing, you're never alone …
K You're never alone with a mobile phone, you're never alone …
P *(laughs)* All right, all right Kelly you can stop that. What *I* really hate is when people shout into them in public places and *every*one has to listen to their boring conversations – you know the kind of thing – er 'Hello sweetheart, it's me. I'm on the train, you can put the dinner in the oven.'
S Sometimes it's not just boring, it's really dangerous, you know, when people use them when they're driving – I've seen lots of …
K And teachers go absolutely mad if we forget to turn them off and they ring in class or you hear the 'beep' 'beep' 'beep' of a text message.
S I'll bet they do. Good manners certainly aren't a wonder of the modern world!
P Well, I have to say for me the most amazing wonder is an obvious one … it's the Internet and email. It's changed the whole world and it's totally transformed *my* business. Everyone at work is always on the computer, checking emails, sending emails. It's where most of our business is done nowadays.
S Yeah, but the bad part is that you're glued to your computer all day – er I reckon people'll forget how to communicate face to face soon, it'll all be through machines. Just because you've got all these different ways to communicate doesn't mean there's any more to say! I'm glad I didn't have emails and texting in my day.
K Ah, but Grandpa, the way things are going, you'll probably be able to send messages through your dishwasher soon!
S Huh, not in my lifetime I hope!

T 1.10 **See p12**

T 1.11

1 food	3 stood	5 read	7 phone
2 near	4 paid	6 work	8 walk

1 **A** Sorry I'm late. I got stuck in traffic.
  B Never mind. You're here now. Come in and sit down.
2 **A** Bye, Mum! I'm off to school now.
  B Take care, my love. Have a nice day!
3 **A** Have you heard that Jenny's going out with Pete?
  B Really? I don't know what she sees in him!
4 **A** How long did it take you to do the homework?
  B Ages! How about you?
5 **A** I don't know about you, but I'm sick and tired of this weather.
  B So am I. I can't stand all this rain.
6 **A** Who was that I saw you with last night?
  B Mind your own business!
7 **A** I'm tired. I'm taking next week off.
  B That sounds like a good idea. The break will do you good.
8 **A** Let's go for a run in the park!
  B Me? Run? You must be joking!
9 **A** Can we get together this afternoon at 3.00?
  B I'm sorry. I can't make it then. What about a bit later?
10 **A** What a gorgeous coat! Was it expensive?
  B Yes, it cost a fortune!

T 1.13

1 I'm taking this Friday and next Monday off. We're going away for a long weekend.
2 Can we meet at about 7 o'clock?
3 I'm really sorry I'm late. I overslept.
4 John's going to take Sue to the party next week.
5 Dad, how much do you earn?

Unit 2

T 2.1 See p15

T 2.2

1 Is he married?
 Yes, he is.
2 What does he do?
 He's a lawyer.
3 Where does he live?
 In a big house in Dallas, Texas.
4 Has he got any children?
 Yes, he's got two.
5 What does his wife do?
 She's an interior designer.
6 Which sports does he play?
 He sometimes plays golf.
7 Where is he working at the moment?
 In Mexico.
8 Is he paid very well?
 Yes, he is.

T 2.3

45-year-old college graduate makes $60,000 a year as a paperboy!

People think it's a joke that a man my age with a college degree is a paperboy! But, hey, it's great. I'm paid good money – $60,000 a year for four hours' work a day. On top of that I often get $50 a week in tips. Not bad!
My job isn't easy. I get up at 2.00 a.m. every day, seven days a week. The first newspaper is delivered at 2.30 a.m. I finish four hours, 65 miles, and 1,000 newspapers later. I drive a red Chevy Blazer and the newspapers are packed into the back.
I love the peace and quiet in the early morning. Most of the time I have the world to myself. Occasionally, I meet a jogger. I usually get back home by 7.00 a.m. Then I have the rest of the day to be with my family and do what I want. I have two teenage children and my wife works at the University of Iowa. Some days I coach my kids' baseball team, other days I play golf. I'm also studying for my master's degree at the moment. I want to be a marriage counsellor eventually, but I'm not in a hurry. I'm enjoying life too much. Some people think it's not much of a job but, hey, when they're sitting in an office, I'm playing golf! So I ask you – who has the better life?

T 2.4

1 I'm paid good money – $60,000 a year. And I often get $50 a week in tips.
2 I get up at 2.00 a.m. … The first newspaper is delivered at 2.30 a.m.
3 I drive a red Chevy Blazer and the newspapers are packed into the back.
4 I love the peace and quiet.
5 Occasionally, I meet a jogger.
6 I usually get back home by 7.00 a.m.
7 My wife works at the University of Iowa.
8 Some days I coach my kids' baseball team, other days I play golf.
9 I'm also studying for my master's degree at the moment. I want to be a marriage counsellor.
10 Some people think it's not much of a job, but, hey, when they're sitting in an office, I'm playing golf.

T 2.5 See p17

T 2.6 Interview with Lucy

I = Interviewer, L = Lucy

1 **I** Do you like your job?
  L Oh yes, I do. I enjoy my job very much.
2 **I** Why do you like it so much?
  L Because I love working with children and making them laugh.
3 **I** What do you wear to work?
  L I wear crazy clothes. A fancy coat and stripy tights.
4 **I** Who are you working with now? Anyone special?
  L Well, at the moment I'm working with a very sick little girl from Bosnia. She's had so many operations. She's very special to me.
5 **I** Does she speak any English?
  L No, she doesn't. We communicate through laughter.
6 **I** Isn't it tiring?
  L Yes, it is. It's very tiring indeed. I'm exhausted at the end of each day.
7 **I** What do you do in the evenings? Do you just go home and relax?
  L No, I don't. I often go out with friends. I have the best friends and the best job in the world.

T 2.7 Sport and leisure

Mary

I'm 85 years old, but I've always been interested in keeping fit. Recently, I started doing aerobics. I go once a week – on – erm – a Thursday morning to the local old people's day centre. It's really nice there. They run a special aerobics class for us. Erm – first thing we do is exercise … for about three quarters of an hour. We go through all the exercises to music. There are between four and eight of us depending on the weather, really. We just wear loose-fitting clothes and comfortable shoes or trainers and, – erm – apart from the music, and Julianne, our lovely instructor, we don't need anything else! I'm quite good at it now. I can do most of the exercises, although there are one or two that are a bit energetic for me at my age – erm – I'm one of the oldest – erm – some of the others are just babies of about sixty! Afterwards we all go for a cup of tea and a piece of cake in the coffee bar. It's a really nice morning.

Jenny

I didn't start skiing until my mid 40s. Now I go once or twice a year for two weeks, usually in early spring. I live in London, so I go to ski resorts in Europe – in France, Italy, or Austria. At first it was really difficult, starting in my 40s. I spent most of my time on my bottom! But I was determined to learn so I took some classes. My husband thought I was mad – but my children said 'You go for it Mum!' so I did and now my husband's taken up skiing, too. I have my own skis, ski poles, and boots and stuff – that I take with me, and of course all the latest clothes – it's important to be fashionable on the ski slopes, you know. I have a lovely ski suit – I like to look good. Now my instructor says I'm a very good skier and in fact I even give lessons to friends – and my husband! If you've never been skiing, you should try it. Hey, I could give you your first lesson!

Thomas

I absolutely love football. I'm crazy about it. It's the best! I love watching it but I 'specially enjoy playing it. I am nine years old and I play for the local team at my school's football pitch. I play matches twice a week – on Friday evenings after school and on Sunday mornings. And we also have football coaching on Tuesday evenings when we just practise all our football skills. It's brilliant! Er – we all have a special kit – a football shirt with a number on the back – er – I'm number 7, it's my lucky number! And we wear shorts, socks and stuff, all in matching colours and of course our football boots – oh – and we also have to wear shin pads for protection, you know. We have a team tracksuit, too – but we only wear this before and after matches and for training. Erm – my mum always comes to support us – even when it's raining. Mmm – my team isn't very good, in fact, we nearly always lose – but we don't care! Er – our football coach, Martin, says winning doesn't matter – it's taking part that counts – mmm – maybe he's right, but d'you know what I think? I think it's just fantastic when we win! Yeah.

T 2.8 See p21

T 2.9 See p21

T 2.10

1 'When are you going away on holiday?'
 'On the fifteenth.'
 'And when do you get back?'

'On the twenty-fourth. I'll give you a ring when we get home.'

2 And now the business news. The unemployment rate has risen slightly this month. The national unemployment rate is now 4.2%, and in our area, an estimated 15,000 people are out of work.

3 'Thank you for calling the Blackpool Concert Hall. This is Matt speaking. How can I help you?'
'Oh, hi. Erm – do you still have seats for tonight's concert?'
'Yes, we do.'
'Great. I'd like two tickets, please. Can I reserve them by phone?'
'Yes, that's fine. Erm – tickets are £35 each. Could I have your name please?'
'Yes, Sarah Dawson.'
'Thanks.'
'Can I pay by visa?'
'Yes that's fine. Erm – what's your card number please?'
'It's 4929 … 7983 … 0621 … 8849.'
'Let me read that back. 4929 … 7983 … 0621 … 8849.'
'That's right.'

4 'Hey, I really like your shoes! Where d'you buy them?'
'At that new shop in town.'
'Oh yeah? Next to the post office.'
'Yeah.'
'How much were they, if you don't mind me asking?'
'£39.99 in the sale. Everything's half price you know, so they were reduced from £79.99.'
'What a bargain!'

5 'Hello?'
'Hi Jim. How're things?'
'Fine. Listen – we're having a party this Saturday, and we were wondering if you'd like to come. It's our tenth wedding anniversary.'
'Congratulations. When is it?'
'It starts at seven o'clock.'
'Saturday at seven? Sounds good.'

Unit 3

T 3.1

The Tale of Gluskap and the Baby

Gluskap the warrior was very pleased with himself because he had fought and won so many battles. He boasted to a woman friend: 'Nobody can beat me!'
'Really?' said the woman. 'I know someone who can beat you. His name is Wasis.' Gluskap had never heard of Wasis. He immediately wanted to meet him and fight him. So he was taken to the woman's village. The woman pointed to a baby who was sitting and sucking a piece of sugar on the floor of a teepee.
'There,' she said. 'That is Wasis. He is little but he is very strong.' Gluskap laughed and went up to the baby. 'I am Gluskap. Fight me!' he shouted. Little Wasis looked at him for a moment, then he opened his mouth. 'Waaah! Waaah!' he screamed. Gluskap had never heard such a terrible noise. He danced a war dance and sang some war songs. Wasis screamed louder. 'Waaah! Waaah! Waaah!' Gluskap covered his ears and ran out of the teepee. After he had run a few miles, he stopped and listened. The baby was still

screaming. Gluskap the fearless was terrified. He ran on and was never seen again in the woman's village.

T 3.2

/t/
laughed
stopped
looked
danced
/d/
covered
listened
opened
screamed
/ɪd/
wanted
shouted
boasted
pointed

T 3.3

1 What was she doing at 7 o'clock yesterday morning?
She was packing her suitcase.
2 What was she doing at 8 o'clock?
She was driving to the airport.
3 What was she doing at 10 o'clock?
She was flying to Glasgow.
4 What was she doing at half past eleven?
She was having a meeting.
5 What was she doing at half past one in the afternoon?
She was having lunch.
6 What was she doing at 3 o'clock?
She was visiting Dot Com Enterprises.
7 What was she doing at 6 o'clock?
She was writing a report on the plane.
8 What was she doing at half past eight in the evening?
She was putting the baby to bed.
9 What was she doing at 10 o'clock?
She was relaxing and listening to music.

T 3.4

1 A I didn't laugh at his joke.
  B Why? Had you heard it before?
2 A Were you surprised by the ending of the film?
  B No, I'd read the book, so I already knew the story.
3 A I went to the airport, but I couldn't get on the plane.
  B Why? Had you left your passport at home?
4 A I was homesick the whole time I was living in France.
  B That's really sad! Had you never lived abroad before?
5 A The hotel where we stayed on holiday was awful!
  B That's a pity. Hadn't you stayed there before?
6 A I met my girlfriend's parents for the first time last Sunday.
  B Really? I thought you'd met them before.
7 A My grandfather had two sons from his first marriage.
  B Really? I didn't know he'd been married before.

T 3.5

An amazing thing happened!

N = Nicola, W = Wanda

N Hi, Wanda. Did you have a good holiday?
W Oh, yeah, we had a great time. But I have to tell you – the most amazing thing happened.
N Really? What was that?
W Well, Roy and I were at the beach near the hotel and we were swimming in the sea – it was our first day – and this huge wave came along and knocked my sunglasses into the water. I …
N Why were you swimming in your sunglasses?
W Oh, I don't know. I'd just left them on top of my head. I'd forgotten they were there. Anyway, they were gone. I couldn't find them anywhere. I was really upset. You know Roy had given me those sunglasses for my birthday and they were really expensive.
N I remember – nearly £100.
W Yeah. Anyway, I had to have sunglasses, so I bought a new pair – just a cheap pair this time. The next day I was lying on the beach, sunbathing. Then, suddenly another huge wave …
N You didn't lose another pair of sunglasses?
W No, no. You'll never believe this – there was another huge wave. It completely covered me. I was so wet and …
N Are you sure this was a good holiday?
W Yeah – but listen! When I looked down, there on the sand, right next to me, were my expensive sunglasses. The ones I had lost the day before! I couldn't believe my eyes!
N You're joking! That is *amazing*!

T 3.6   **Books and films**

V = Vinnie, W=Will, S = Sue, M = Maeve,

V Hey, I just read a great book.
W A book? Hey Vinnie, we're impressed! What was it?
V *The Philosopher's Stone*
M Isn't that a Harry Potter book?
V Well, yeah, yeah, but … . No, no, come on you guys, – really, it was terrific. I was so amazed. JK Rowling's a really good writer. Lots of adults read her books, they're not just for kids.
W Sure, Vinnie. You believe that, if you want.
S No, come on, he's right. I mean, I've seen people reading Harry Potter on the Underground and I've seen the video – my nephew has it – it's excellent!
M Actually, I've just bought *Captain Corelli's Mandolin* on DVD. Has anyone read that book?
S Oh no, no, please! Not *Captain Corelli's Mandolin*. I could *not* read that book. Everybody said it was great. I could *not* read it.
W You have to skip the first hundred pages and after that it's great.
V Hey guys! Call me old-fashioned but I like to begin a book at the beginning.
W But it is a great story, though – 'specially when it, y'know, moves to him and the girl on the Greek island.
M Yeah, it's a fantastic love story. But sooo sad! Actually, I read it on holiday, on a beach on a

Greek island – would you believe – and I just cried and cried. People kept asking me if I was OK!

V Hey, didn't Nick Cage star in the film?

W Yeah, with Penelope Cruz … she is just so lovely …

M Er well right so …what *is* your favourite book then Sue?

S Oh … well … my all time best is … right, you'll never believe this … it's – it's *Dracula!*

M *Dracula?* You're kidding!

S No – no, I'm not. I know everybody's *heard* of *Dracula* and *seen Dracula* films, but I bet not many people have read the book. It's by a man called Bram Stoker and it's brilliant.

W Yeah – there are loads of *Dracula* films. Er, I saw one not long ago actually, with – er – Tom Cruise.

V Yeah, yeah, I love horror movies – the scarier the better!

M Well, actually, I think *Frankenstein's* a much better horror movie. You feel really sorry for that poor monster.

S Well, it's good but not that good. I mean that's only *my* opinion of course.

V *Dracula* is more scary … with huge teeth that he sinks into the necks of beautiful women. Aaargh!

M Aaargh! That's disgusting!

S OK Vinney. OK. So what else do *you* read – I mean other than Harry Potter that is?

V Hey – come on, come on! I had to read Ernest Hemingway at school and I quite enjoyed it … oh … what was it called? Oh yeah, yeah, yeah, *The Sun Also Sets*

W *Rises.* – *The Sun Also Rises.*

V Whatever.

W No I read it years ago – it's a great read, actually. It's all about Hemingway's travels through France and Spain, isn't it? Oh, … and his drinking.

M Yeah, Hemingway drank a lot, didn't he? Well, we're going on holiday to Florida next month. Maybe we can hang out in the bars where he used to drink and …

V What? What? Hemingway lived in Florida?!

W You're the American!

V Well …

W Yeah, in – in Key West, but we'll only visit *some* of the bars he went to!

T 3.7

1 **A** Did you like the film?
  B It was excellent. Have you seen it yet? It stars Julia Kershaw and Antonio Bellini.
2 **A** What did you think of the play?
  B It was really boring! I fell asleep during the first act.
3 **A** Did you like your pizzas?
  B They were delicious. John had tomato and mozzarella and I had tuna and sweetcorn.
4 **A** Do you like Malcolm Baker's novels?
  B I didn't like his first one, but I couldn't put his latest one down until the last page.
5 **A** What do you think of their children?
  B I think they spoil them. They always give them whatever they want.
6 **A** What was your holiday like?
  B It was a nice break, but the weather wasn't very good.
7 **A** What did you think of Sally Cotter?

  B She's usually good, but I don't think she was right for this part.
8 **A** What was the match like?
  B It was really exciting, especially when David Stuart scored in the closing minutes.

Unit 4

T 4.1 Teenagers and parents

I = Interviewer, **S** = Sarah, **L** = Lindsay

I Tell me, what are some good things about being a teenager and not an adult?

S Um … well, for one thing, you don't have to go to work.

L Yeah. And you don't have to pay bills.

I OK …

L And you can go out with your friends, and you can go shopping, and you can go to the cinema, and you can …

S Oh, come on, Lindsay. Adults can do all that too! But what's different is how much freedom teenagers have.

L Don't have, you mean.

S Right. How much freedom we don't have. I mean, I always have to tell my mum and dad where I'm going and what time I'm coming home.

L Mmm.

I And what time do you have to get back home?

S Mmm – by 10 o'clock on a week-day, maybe 11 or 12 at the weekend.

L It doesn't matter because you never have enough money anyway!

S Definitely. You get pocket money from your parents, but it's never enough. And you aren't allowed to buy whatever you want.

I OK, OK. Life's tough for kids, but what do you think it's like being an adult? Lindsay?

L Well, adults have to worry about paying the bills and taking care of their family. They can't always do what they want when they want.

I They have responsibilities, you mean?

L Yeah. I feel more sorry for my mum than my dad. She's always rushing around and she has to go to work as well. She doesn't have to work on Thursdays and Fridays, but she still has loads of different things to do in a day, like shopping and cooking, and taking me to dance classes.

I So, do you think your dad has an easier life?

L Well, I don't know. He has to drive over 500 miles a week.

I Sarah, tell me about school. What are some of the rules at your school?

S Oh! There are so many! Let's see. We can't wear make-up. We aren't allowed to chew gum. We aren't allowed to bring mobile phones to class . . .

L There are millions of rules – all of them stupid.

S And if you break one of the rules, you have to stay after school!

L Well, speaking of school, I've got to go. I've got to do my homework!

T 4.2

1 You don't have to go to work.
2 You don't have to pay bills.
3 You can go out with your friends.

---

4 I always have to tell my mum and dad where I'm going.
5 What time do you have to get back home?
6 You aren't allowed to buy whatever you want.
7 Adults have to worry about paying the bills.
8 They can't always do what they want.
9 We aren't allowed to bring mobile phones to class.
10 I've got to go. I've got to do my homework.

T 4.3

1 Where's my briefcase? I've got to go to work!
2 Look at those dirty plates! We've got to do the washing-up.
3 Pamela and Charles don't have any food in their house. They've got to go shopping.
4 John needs to get an alarm clock. He's got to get up early tomorrow.
5 I haven't got any clean socks. I've got to do the washing.
6 The chef's ill, so the waiter's got to do the cooking.

T 4.4 See p32

T 4.5 See p33

T 4.6 **G**=Grandma, **A** = Antony

G You must look after your money.
A Yes, Grandma! I will.
G You mustn't talk to strangers.
A No, Grandma! I won't.
G You mustn't go out when it's dark.
A No, Grandma! I won't.
G You mustn't drink too much beer.
A No, Grandma! I won't.
G You must make sure you eat well.
A Yes, Grandma! I will.
G You must have a bath regularly.
A Yes, Grandma! I will.
G You must phone us if you're in trouble.
A Yes, Grandma! I will.
G You mustn't go anywhere that's dangerous.
A No, Grandma! I won't.

T 4.7 A new job

D = Dave, **M** = Manager

D So, um … what time do I have to start?
M 11.00 in the morning or 4.00 in the afternoon.
D And do I have to wear a uniform?
M Definitely. You have to wear the same uniform as everyone else – a short-sleeved white shirt, black trousers, and a red hat. And a name tag.
D So … what do I do exactly?
M You serve the customers. Remember – you must always be polite. You say 'Good morning' or whatever the time of day, and then 'Can I help you?' When they tell you what they want, you have to enter it into the computer, and when they're finished, you should read back what they've ordered. Then you take their money, and you put together their food. That's it.
D Great. When can I start?
M You start at 4.00 tomorrow afternoon.
D Cool.
M Here's your hat. And your name tag. You're all set. Welcome to Burger Heaven, Dave.

T 4.8

The Italians eat a lot of pasta.
The Chinese cook lots of noodles and rice.

The British invented football.
The Canadians often watch ice hockey on TV.
The French produce champagne.
The Japanese eat raw fish.
The Scots wear kilts on special occasions.

T 4.9 **Come round to my place!**

Sumie

My name is Sumie. I come from Nagano, Japan. In my country, we usually invite guests home at the weekend for dinner, at about 7 o'clock in the evening. Before they come, we must tidy the front garden and clean the entrance hall. Then we must spray it all with water to show that we welcome our guests with cleanliness. The guests usually bring a gift, and when they give you the gift they say, 'I'm sorry this is such a small gift,' but in fact they have chosen it very carefully. When the meal is ready the hostess says, 'We have nothing special for you today, but you are welcome to come this way'. You can see that in Japan you should try to be modest and you should not show off too much. If you don't understand our culture, you may think this is very strange. When we have foreign guests, we try to serve traditional Japanese meals like sushi, tempura, or sukiyaki, but when we have Japanese guests, we serve all kinds of food such as spaghetti, Chinese food, or steaks.
When guests leave, the host and hostess see them out of the house and wait until their car turns the corner of the street; they wait until they can't see them any more.

Kate

My name is Kate and I'm from Bristol in England. We like to have people over for lunch and they usually get here around noon. We often have people over to eat, but sometimes when we invite a lot of people over, for a family gathering for example, we have what's called a 'potluck lunch'.
A potluck is an informal occasion, so people dress casually. If the weather is nice we'll have it outside in the garden. What makes it fun is that everyone who comes has to bring a dish of food. They're given a choice: starter, main course, salad or vegetable, or dessert. As the host, I'll know how many of each kind of dish the guests will bring, but not exactly what the foods will be. That's why it's called 'potluck' – it's a surprise, having a dinner party and not knowing what you're going to feed the guests! All I have to do is make one dish myself and get cups, glasses, and knives and forks together, and supply the drinks. As the guests arrive, they put their dish on the table, and people help themselves. Some guests might bring a bottle of wine or flowers as a gift but I don't expect anything. It's a fun, relaxed way of getting together with friends or family.

Lucas

My name is Lucas and I'm from Porto Alegre which is in the southern part of Brazil. We like to invite our friends over at weekends, on a Friday or a Saturday night for a 'Churrasco', or Brazilian barbecue. These are very popular in this part of Brazil.
People come about 8.00 in the evening and stay to midnight or even later – sometimes until 2.00 in the morning, whenever people start getting sleepy. People stay a long time; there is no set time for dinner to end. We'll sit around and play cards or just talk. It's very informal. If people

want to bring something, I'll tell them to bring something for the meal like a bottle of wine or something for dessert.
Ah, but what about the food? At a 'Churrasco', we cook different kinds of meat on long metal skewers over an open flame. We have all kinds of meat: beef, pork, and maybe Brazilian sausage. Sometimes chicken too. Then we cut off slices of meat from the skewers to serve the guests. It's really delicious. We usually have potato salad or rice as side dishes. After the meal we drink coffee or espresso.

T 4.10

1 A Could you bring us the bill, please?
  B Yes, sir. I'll bring it right away.
2 A Would you give me your work number, please?
  B Of course. Oh, shall I give you my mobile number, too?
3 A Can I help you?
  B Just looking, thanks.
4 A Two large coffees, please.
  B White or black?
5 A Can you tell me the code for Paris, please?
  B One moment. I'll look it up.
6 A I'll give you a lift if you like.
  B That would be great! Could you drop me off at the library?
7 A Would you mind opening the window?
  B No problem. It's stuffy in here.
8 A Could I have extension 238, please?
  B That line's engaged. Would you like to hold?

T 4.11

1 'So, anyway, there I was, sitting in my boss's office. All of a sudden, the phone rings and my boss says …'
  'Sorry to interrupt, darling, but I think the baby's crying. Could you go and check?'
2 'Can I help you?'
  'Yes, I bought these shoes here two days ago, and the heel on this one is already broken. Can I change them for a new pair?'
  'Of course. Let me see if we have another pair in your size.'
3 'Will you turn down that awful music?'
  'What?'
  'Will you turn down that awful music? Or better still – turn it off!'
  'Oh, all right.'
4 'Hi, Bob. Where are you going?'
  'I have a meeting with the web designer and the programmer about our new website this afternoon.'
  'Could you do me a favour? Would you mind asking the programmer to call me? I have a question for him about the budget.'
  'Sure. No problem.'

Unit 5

T 5.1 **Ben's list**

B = Ben, A = Alice

B I'm going shopping. Do we need anything?
A I don't think so. … Oh, hang on. We haven't got any sugar.
B It's OK. It's on my list. I'm going to buy some.
A What about bread?
B Good idea! I'll get a loaf.

A Er, what time will you be back?
B I don't know. I might stop at Nick's. It depends on how much time I've got.
A Don't forget we're playing tennis with Dave and Donna this afternoon.
B Don't worry. I won't forget. I'll be back before then.
A OK.

T 5.2 **What's going to happen?**

1 A Have you got the plane tickets?
  B Yes. They're with the passports and traveller's cheques.
  A What time is the taxi coming?
  B In about thirty minutes. What's the name of the hotel we're staying at?
  A The Grand Hotel.
  B Have you remembered your swimming costume this year?
  A Oh, yes. It's packed. What about tennis rackets?
  B I put them in my case, with the fifteen books.
  A Right. Let's get these cases closed.

2 A Well, darling, it's our big day soon.
  B I know. I can't wait. I hope the weather's good.
  A Yes, it makes such a difference, doesn't it?
  B The church is looking beautiful.
  A And the hotel's getting ready for the reception.
  B And then there's our honeymoon in Rome.
  A Ah!

3 A Have you packed the books and the pictures from the living room?
  B Yes. And all the kitchen things are packed, too.
  A That's it then. What time are the removal men coming?
  B Early, I hope. About 7.00 in the morning.
  A Good. It's a long drive, *and* it's right in the middle of the countryside.
  B I can't wait to be there.
  A And I can't wait to get the baby's room ready.
  B Tom if it's a boy and Natalie if it's a girl. How exciting!

T 5.3

1 I think Jerry will win the tennis match. He's been playing really well lately.
2 I think it'll be a nice day tomorrow. The forecast is for warm and dry weather.
3 I think I'll pass my exam on Friday. I've been studying for weeks.
4 I think you'll like the film. It's a wonderful story, and the acting is excellent.
5 I think we'll get to the airport in time. But we'd better get going.
6 I think you'll get the job. You have the right qualifications and plenty of experience.

T 5.4

1 I don't think Jerry will win the tennis match. He hasn't practised for weeks.
2 I don't think it'll be a nice day tomorrow. The forecast said rainy and windy.
3 I don't think I'll pass my exam on Friday. I haven't studied at all.
4 I don't think you'll like the film. It's a bit boring.
5 I don't think we'll get to the airport in time.

There's too much traffic.

6 I don't think you'll get the job. They're looking for someone with more experience.

T 5.5 Arranging to meet

L = Liz, MY = Min Young

L We need to meet some time this weekend to talk about our project.

MY OK. What are you doing today?

L Well, this afternoon I've got a dance class, but I'm not doing anything this evening. What about you?

MY Mmm – I'm going shopping this afternoon, and this evening I'm going ice-skating. What about tomorrow?

L Well, I'm having my hair cut tomorrow afternoon, so that'll take a while.

MY What time will you be finished at the hairdresser's?

L About 4 o'clock. What are you doing around that time?

MY I don't know. I might be free.

L OK. Why don't we meet at the Internet Café at about 5 o'clock? We can have a coffee and do our work.

MY Sounds good to me. Are you going out in the evening?

L Yes. I'm going out for dinner with a couple of friends. Do you want to join us?

MY That would be great! I'd love to.

L OK. So we'll meet tomorrow at 5 o'clock at the Internet Café.

MY Good.

T 5.6 A weather forecast

And here's the weather for some popular destinations in Western Europe for the next twenty-four hours.

A Let's begin in the north. I'm afraid spring isn't here yet! Another major frontal system will move in from the Atlantic affecting Northern Ireland and Scotland, before moving on to Scandinavia. It's going to bring plenty of rain, which could fall as snow on Scottish mountains. So it will feel very chilly everywhere. Temperatures around five or six degrees at best in the rain but much lower in snowy areas, where they will stay around freezing all day, you'll be lucky to see two degrees.

B Moving south now, into England and Wales, most of northern France, and across through Belgium and Holland. Things look more springlike here and it will be a lot brighter than in recent weeks. Along Channel coasts especially, there may be a little rain at first, with temperatures reaching only eight degrees. Inland, however, there will be more sunshine than showers, with all areas becoming warmer and drier as the day goes on. Towards the end of the day temperatures could be as high as 15 degrees in these regions. The winds will be light, coming from the south but it will feel very pleasant.

C If you're lucky enough to be going to southern France or Spain you'll find the best of today's weather. In the far south of Spain, mainly clear skies, lots of sun with high temperatures for the time of year up to 24 degrees, and everywhere else 18 or 19 degrees with some cloud. But it's not all good news. Strong winds along the southern French coast could spoil your evening walk.

D Further east, across the Alps, from Switzerland into northern Italy, there are the remains of another weather system. There will be stormy weather during the day with thunder and lightning, bringing over two inches of rain to some lowland areas and heavy snow to the mountains. Strong winds and rain will continue most of the day. The winds will make it feel much cooler for the time of year with temperatures struggling to reach ten degrees. And watch out for early morning fog.

So that's it, a quick tour of Western Europe – not bad in central countries, warm and sunny in Spain; cool, wet, and windy in parts of Italy, and Switzerland – oh, and stay away from those Scottish mountains unless you're wearing warm clothes.

T 5.7

1 A Do you think it'll be a rough crossing?
  B Well, the forecast is good, so it should be pretty smooth.
2 A Excuse me, I think those seats facing the front are ours.
  B Oh, I'm sorry. We didn't know they were reserved.
3 A We're going to Market Street. Could you tell us when it's our stop?
  B Just sit near the front and I'll call it out.
4 A Can you take us to the airport?
  B Of course. Hop in!
5 A Can I take these bags on with me?
  B I'm sorry. Only one item of hand luggage per passenger.
6 A That's all right. You can keep the change.
  B Thanks a lot. Do you want a hand with those bags?
7 A Excuse me, are we landing on time?
  B Yes. We're beginning our descent soon.
8 A No, no! He said turn *left* at the lights, not right!
  B Look! *You* drive and *I'll* give directions from now on! Right?`
9 A How do I get to Oxford Circus?
  B Take the Piccadilly Line, eastbound, and change at Green Park.

Unit 6

T 6.1 A student visitor

S = Sandy, N = Nina

S Our student from Seoul arrived on Monday.
N What's her name?
S Soon-hee.
N That's a pretty name! What's she like?
S She's really nice. I'm sure we'll get on well. We seem to have a lot in common.
N How do you know that already? What does she like doing?
S Well, she likes dancing, and so do I. And we both like listening to the same kind of music.
N What does she look like?
S Oh, she's really pretty. She has big, brown eyes and long, dark hair.
N Why don't we do something with Soon-hee this weekend? What should we do? Get a pizza? Go clubbing? What would she like to do?
S I'll ask her tonight. She was a bit homesick at first, so I'm pretty sure she'll want to go out and make some friends.
N How is she now?

S Oh, she's OK. She called her parents and she felt much better after she'd spoken to them.
N Oh, that's good. I can't wait to meet her.

T 6.2

1 Thai food? It's delicious. It can be spicy, but it doesn't have to be.
2 Oh, she's very nice. You'd really like her. She's the kind of person you can always go to with a problem.
3 Not very well. He still has a temperature and a bad cough.
4 Well, she's crazy about horses. I don't think she has any other hobbies. Oh, she plays golf sometimes.
5 It's not very nice at all. It's raining, it's cold, and it's pretty miserable. What about where you are?
6 Mmm … a little like you, as a matter of fact. He's about the same height, tall with blond hair, but your hair's longer and straighter than his. Other than that, you two are quite similar.
7 It was great. Really relaxing. Lots of sunshine, good food. We did almost nothing but sit by the pool and read books for the whole two weeks.
8 I like all kinds, but I suppose I like biographies and detective stories best.

T 6.3 A thank-you letter

Dear Sandy and family,
I just wanted to say thank you for having me as your guest in your beautiful home. I had a great time. I really enjoyed meeting your friends. You all made me feel so welcome. You know how much I missed my family at first, but you were so kind that I soon stopped feeling homesick. I can't find the words to tell you how grateful I am. I'd like to call you. What's a good time to call?
You know that on my way home I stopped to visit my aunt in Perth. It was so hot! It was over 35 degrees all the time but I absolutely loved it. My aunt wanted me to stay longer, but I wanted to see my parents and my brother, Sang-chul. But she's invited me to go back and I'd love to do that. I'm thinking of going next year.
Anyway, I'm looking forward to hearing from you very soon. Let me know if you ever want to visit Seoul. My brother and I could take you to a 'norebang' (a singing room). It's a bit like karaoke!
Love to you all,
Soon-hee
P.S. Do you like the picture of Sang-chul and me?

T 6.4

1 They promised to bring the wine.
2 The teacher told them to do their homework.
3 I've just finished answering my emails.
4 Don't forget to take your passport.
5 He finally succeeded in passing his driving test.
6 We asked him to move his car.
7 I just need to go to the loo. I'll be back in a minute.
8 I don't mind looking after your cat.
9 Just let me finish what I'm saying.
10 Please can you help me carry this upstairs?
11 I hate shopping for clothes.
12 She's really looking forward to working with us.

T 6.6

1 A Nick's really quiet and shy. He never says a word.
   B Yeah, his brother is much more outgoing.
2 A What's Carrie's boyfriend like?
   B Well, he's tall, dark and handsome, but he's not very polite. In fact, he's even ruder than Carrie!
3 A How was your lunch?
   B Ugh! It was awful. The pizza was disgusting. We were really starving, but we still couldn't eat it!
4 A Mmm! These tomatoes are really delicious. Did you grow them yourselves?
   B Yes, we did. All our vegetables are home-grown.
5 A Did you have a good time in London?
   B We had a great time. There's so much to do. It's a really exciting city. And there are so many people from all over the world. I think it's nearly as cosmopolitan as New York.

T 6.7 New York

I = Interviewer, J = Justin, C = Cinda

I How long have you been here in New York?
J Nearly three years.
I And are you enjoying it?
J We love it.
C It's great.
I So what do you like best?
C Oh, the atmosphere, the mixture of all kinds of people. The speed of everything – it's exciting.
J I love the architecture, it's so different from London. Walking the streets and looking up at all those skyscrapers.
I And what about the people?
C Well, New Yorkers have a reputation for being rude and unfriendly, but I don't think that's true. People are always in a hurry, but they're not unfriendly.
J What I love is the – the great mixture of nationalities and cultures. It's got to be the most cosmopolitan city in the world.
I More than London?
J Hmm … well, I think so, but they're both very mixed.
C Life here seems much faster than in London. Everyone's in such a rush. Everything's done for speed. For example, I – I don't think people cook at home much – everyone seems to eat out or get food delivered because it's quicker and easier.
I Have you made many friends here?
J I've made friends at work mostly. But it's – it's difficult to make friends outside of work – people are so busy. But mostly I find people pretty friendly.
C Except the taxi drivers! Some of the rudest people I've ever met are New York taxi drivers!
J And some of the worst drivers. Every time I sit in a taxi I say a prayer. They drive so fast and suddenly they change lanes. And worst of all they don't seem to know where anything is.
C Yeah – you spend the entire journey giving directions. Anyway, I like using the subway. It's cheap.
J Yeah, and easy to use and it seems safe to me. We walk a lot as well. It's a lot safer now than

it was ten years ago. It's still not very clean but it's getting better.
I Do you have a car?
J No. No, we don't. Not many of our friends do, actually. You don't really need one.
C I'd hate to drive in the city, I'd be terrified. Anyway, you can get everything delivered to your door – not just food.
I Don't you go shopping?
J Oh yeah, of course we do. Not all of us can afford to shop on 5th Avenue, you know, but it's – it's fun to look.
C Actually, the shops – sorry, the stores – are great. Always open – well nearly always – til 9.00 or 10.00 at night.
J People work much later here. I wasn't expecting to work such long hours! And the holidays – sorry, vacation time – and the – the public holidays they're, they're much shorter. I only get ten days a year. It's difficult for people like us with families in other countries. It's difficult to find time to visit them.
I But generally you're happy?
J Fantastic!
C It's an amazing place, but in a few years I think I'll be exhausted and ready for a quieter life!

T 6.8 London

I = Interviewer, A = Alan

I Alan, how long have you lived in London?
A Fifteen years.
I And do you like it here?
A Sure I like it – but London is one of those cities that you love and hate at the same time.
I So first – what do you hate?
A Oh the usual big city things – the crowds, the dirt, the traffic, and of course the Underground – it's so expensive compared with the subway in New York.
I And what do you like?
A Oh, a lot: fantastic theatres – I'm an actor so that's important for me – great art galleries, museums, I love the Natural History Museum. Concerts, wonderful orchestras. The best of everything comes to London.
I And what's best for you?
A For me? Oh, I just love standing on Waterloo Bridge and looking down the river at the Houses of Parliament and now, of course there's the London Eye – I think it's just wonderful. And – I like travelling in the black cabs. Taxi drivers here are great, so friendly! They tell you their life stories AND they know every street in London – not like in New York.
I And what about the people? What do you think of Londoners?
A Ah well – generally speaking, I think that they do live up to their reputation – they are reserved. It takes a while to get to know people. They won't tell you about themselves. You say to an American 'How are you?' and you get 'Oh man, I'm just great. I got the promotion and I love working here in Dallas, Denver, Detroit or Delaware etc. y' know. Ask an Englishman 'How are you?' and you get 'Er – fine, thank you'.
I So the stereotype's true?
A Yeah, they're – they're pretty reserved. They don't like giving personal details, but they complain a lot about life generally. They seem much less positive about life – much more

cynical than Americans. They grumble about transport and politicians and money, how much things cost, their work …
I So, we're a miserable lot then!
A Not really. Leisure time – sorry – free time – is really important to the British. I think for many Americans, work is the most important thing in their lives. Americans work much longer hours. In Britain they get more vacation time and time off …
I … and still they grumble!
A Yeah.
I You've been in London 15 years. Has it changed in that time?
A Oh yeah a lot – especially the shops, they stay open much longer now. They used to close every Wednesday afternoon. People in the States could never believe that. Oh and the food!
I Everyone says English food is terrible. Is it?
A Well, when I first came it was terrible. It was so hard to get good food. Nowadays it's not hard at all. London has some great restaurants – my favourite here is the Indian food, it's fantastic. I think we have one of the best right here on our street. Just the best!
I You live in south London. Do you like it there?
A Very much. I love the mix of cultures and nationalities in every street.
I How long do you think you'll stay here?
A Oh, I don't know. Maybe five more years. Maybe forever!

Grammar Reference

UNIT 1

Introduction to auxiliary verbs

There are three classes of verbs in English.

1 The auxiliary verbs *do*, *be*, and *have*
These are used to form tenses, and to show forms such as questions and negatives.

2 Modal auxiliary verbs
Must, can, should, might, will, and *would* are examples of modal auxiliary verbs. They 'help' other verbs, but unlike *do, be*, and *have*, they have their own meanings. For example, *must* expresses obligation and *can* expresses ability. (See Units 4, 5, 8, and 9.)

3 Full verbs
These are all the other verbs in the language, for example, *play, run, help, think, want, go*, etc.
Do, be, and *have* can also be used as full verbs with their own meanings.

do
I **do** *my washing on Saturdays.*
She **does** *a lot of business in Eastern Europe.*
What **do** *you* **do**? = *What's your job?* (The first *do* is an auxiliary; the second is a full verb.)

be
We **are** *in class at the moment.*
They **were** *at home yesterday.*
I want **to be** *a teacher.*

have
He **has** *a lot of problems.*
They **have** *three children.*

A note on *have* and *have got*

There are two forms of the verb *have: have* as a full verb with *do/does/did* for questions, negatives, and short answers and *have got* where *have* is an auxiliary.

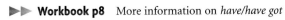 **Workbook p8** More information on *have/have got*

1.1 Tenses and auxiliary verbs

When *do, be*, and *have* are used as auxiliary verbs, they make different verb forms.

do

In the Present Simple and the Past Simple there is no auxiliary verb, so *do, does*, and *did* are used to make questions and negatives (except with *be / have got*).

Where **do** *you work?*
She **doesn't** *like her job.*
What **did** *you buy?*
We **didn't** *buy anything.*

be

1 *Be* + verb + *-ing* is used to make continuous verb forms. Continuous verb forms describe activities in progress and temporary activities.
He's **washing** *his hair.* (Present Continuous)
They **were going** *to work.* (Past Continuous)
I've **been learning** *English for two years.* (Present Perfect Continuous)
I'd like **to be lying** *on the beach right now.* (Continuous infinitive)

2 *Be* + past participle is used to form the passive.
Paper **is made** *from wood.* (Present Simple passive)
My car **was stolen** *yesterday.* (Past Simple passive)
The house **has been** *redecorated.* (Present Perfect passive)
This homework needs **to be done** *tonight.* (Passive infinitive)
There is an introduction to the passive on p74.

have

Have + past participle is used to make perfect verb forms.
He **has worked** *in seven different countries.* (Present Perfect)
She was crying because she **had had** *some bad news.* (Past Perfect)
I'd like to **have met** *Napoleon.* (Perfect infinitive)

Perfect means 'before,' so Present Perfect means 'before now.' (See Units 7 and 10.) Past Perfect means 'before a time in the past.' (See Unit 3.)

1.2 Negatives and auxiliary verbs

To make a negative, add *-n't* to the auxiliary verb. If there is no auxiliary verb, use *don't/doesn't/didn't*.

Positive	Negative
He's working.	*He* **isn't** *working.*
I was thinking.	*I* **wasn't** *thinking.*
We've seen the play.	*We* **haven't** *seen the play.*
She works in a bank.	*She* **doesn't** *work in a bank.*
They like skiing.	*They* **don't** *like skiing.*
He went on holiday.	*He* **didn't** *go on holiday.*

It is possible to contract the auxiliaries *be* and *have* and use the uncontracted *not*.
He's **not** *playing today.* (= He *isn't* playing today.)
We're **not** *going to Italy after all.* (= We *aren't* going to Italy …)
I've **not** *read that book yet.* (= I *haven't* read the book yet.)
But
I'm **not** *working.*   NOT   ~~I amn't working.~~

1.3 Questions and auxiliary verbs

1 To make a question, invert the subject and the auxiliary verb.
If there is no auxiliary verb, use *do/does/did*.

	Question
She's wearing jeans.	*What **is she** wearing?*
You aren't working.	*Why **aren't you** working?*
You were born in Paris.	*Where **were you** born?*
Peter's been to China.	***Has Peter** been to China?*
We have been studying.	***Have you** been studying?*
I know you.	***Do I** know you?*
He wants ice-cream.	*What **does he** want?*
They didn't go out.	*Why **didn't they** go out?*

2 There is usually no *do/does/did* in subject questions. Compare:

Who wants ice-cream?	*What flavour ice-cream **do** you want?*
What happened to your eye?	*What **did** you do to your eye?*
Who broke the window?	*How **did** you break the window?*

1.4 Short answers and auxiliary verbs

Short answers are very common in spoken English. If you just say *Yes*
or *No*, it can sound rude. We use short answers after *Yes / No* questions.
To make a short answer, repeat the auxiliary verb. In the Present and
Past Simple, use *do/does/did*.

	Short answer
Are you coming with us?	*Yes, **I am**.*
Have you had breakfast?	*No, **I haven't**.*
Kate likes walking.	*No, **she doesn't**. She hates it.*
Mary didn't phone.	*Yes, **she did**. You were out.*
Don't forget to write.	*No, **I won't**.*

UNIT 2

2.1 Present Simple

Form

Positive and negative

I We You They	work. don't work.
He She It	works. doesn't work.

Question

Where	do	I we you they	live?
	does	he she it	

Do you live in Bristol?
Does he have a car?

Short answer
*Yes, **we do**.*
*No, **he doesn't**.*

Use

The Present Simple is used to express:

1 an action that happens again and again (a habit).
*I **go** to work by car.*
*She **drinks** ten cups of coffee a day.*
*I **wash** my hair twice a week.*

2 a fact that is always true.
*Ronaldo **comes** from Brazil.*
*Some birds **fly** south in winter.*
*My daughter **has** brown eyes.*

3 a fact that is true for a long time (a state).
*He **works** in a bank.*
*I **live** in a flat near the centre of town.*
*I **prefer** coffee to tea.*

Spelling of verb + -s

1 Most verbs add *-s* to the base form of the verb.
wants   eats   helps   drives

2 Add *-es* to verbs that end in *-ss*, *-sh*, *-ch*, *-x*, and *-o*.
kisses   washes   watches   fixes   goes

3 Verbs that end in a consonant + *-y* change the *-y* to *-ies*.
carries   flies   worries   tries

But verbs that end in a vowel + *-y* only add *-s*.
buys   says   plays   enjoys

▶▶ **Workbook p14**   Pronunciation of *-s* at the end of a word

Adverbs of frequency

1 We often use adverbs of frequency with the Present Simple.

0%			50%			100%
never	rarely	not often	sometimes	often	usually	always

2 They go before the main verb, but after the verb *be*. Compare:

*I **usually** start school at 9.00.*	*They're **usually** in a hurry in the morning.*
*I don't **often** go to bed late.*	*I'm not **often** late for school.*
*She **never** eats meat.*	*He's **never** late.*
*I **rarely** see Peter these days.*	*We're **rarely** at home at the weekends.*

3 *Sometimes* and *usually* can also go at the beginning or the end.
Sometimes *we play cards.*   *We play cards* **sometimes**.
Usually *I go shopping with friends.*   *I go shopping with friends* **usually**.

Never, always, rarely, and *seldom* cannot move in this way.

NOT   ~~Never I go to the movies.~~
       ~~Always I have tea in the morning.~~

4 *Every day*, etc., goes at the end.
He phones me **every night**.

 2.2 Present Continuous

Form

Positive and negative

I	'm 'm not	
He/She/It	's isn't	eating.
We/You/They	're aren't	

Question

What	am is are	I he/she/it we/you/they	doing?

Short answer

Are you going by train?	Yes, I am. No, I'm not.

Use

The Present Continuous is used to express:

1 an activity that is happening now.
Don't turn the TV off. I'm **watching** *it.*
You can't speak to Lisa. She's **having** *a bath.*

2 an activity or situation that is true now, but is not necessarily happening at the moment of speaking.
Don't take that book. Jane's **reading** *it.*
I'm **doing** *a French evening class this year.*

3 a temporary activity.
Peter is a student, but he's **working** *as a waiter during the holidays.*
I'm **living** *with friends until I find a place of my own.*

4 a planned future arrangement.
I'm **having** *lunch with Glenda tomorrow.*
We're **meeting** *at 1.00 outside the restaurant.*

Spelling of verb + -ing

1 Most verbs add *-ing* to the base form of the verb.
going   wearing   visiting   eating

2 Verbs that end in one *-e* lose the *-e.*
smoking   coming   hoping   writing
Verbs that end in *-ee* don't drop an *-e.*
agreeing   seeing

❶ *lie   lying*

3 Verbs of one syllable, with one vowel and one consonant, double the consonant.
stopping   getting   running   planning   jogging
If the final consonant is *-y* or *-w*, it is not doubled.
playing   showing

2.3 State verbs

1 There are certain groups of verbs that are usually only used in the Present Simple. This is because their meanings are related to states or conditions that are facts and not activities. This is a feature of the use of the Present Simple. The groups of verbs are:

Verbs of thinking and opinions

believe	think	understand	suppose	expect
agree	doubt	know	remember	forget
mean	imagine	realize	deserve	prefer

I **believe** *you.*
Do *you* **understand**?
I **know** *his face, but I* **forget** *his name.*

Verbs of emotions and feelings

like	love	hate	care	hope	wish	want	admit

I **like** *black coffee.*
Do *you* **want** *to go out?*
I **don't care**.

Verbs of having and being

belong	own	have	possess	contain	cost	seem	appear
need	depend on	weigh	come from	resemble			

This book **belongs** *to Jane.*
How much **does** *it* **cost**?
He **has** *a lot of money.*

Verbs of the senses

look	hear	taste	smell	feel

The food **smells** *good.*

We often use *can* when the subject is a person.
Can *you smell something burning?*
I **can** *hear someone crying.*

2 Some of these verbs can be used in the Present Continuous, but with a change of meaning. In the continuous, the verb expresses an activity, not a state. Compare:

I **think** *you're right.* (opinion)	*We're* **thinking** *of going to the cinema.* (mental activity)
He **has** *a lot of money.* (possession)	*She's* **having** *a bad day.* (activity)
I **see** *what you mean.* (understand)	*Are you* **seeing** *Nigel tomorrow?* (activity)
The soup **tastes** *awful.* (state)	*I'm* **tasting** *the soup to see if it needs salt.* (activity)

Introduction to the passive

The passive is dealt with in Units 2, 3, and 7.

Form

to be + past participle

The tense of the verb *to be* changes to give different tenses in the passive. Compare:

*A party **is being held** by the Patels next week.* (Present Continuous passive)
*My neighbour **is invited** to their party every year.* (Present Simple passive)
*He **was invited** last year, I wasn't.* (Present Perfect passive)
*I'd love **to be invited** to their party.* (Passive infinitive)

Use

1 Passive sentences move the focus from the subject to the object of active sentences.
   *Alfred Hitchcock **directed** Psycho in 1960.*
   *Psycho, one of the classic thrillers of all time, **was directed** by Alfred Hitchcock.*

   The passive is not just another way of expressing the same sentence in the active. We choose the active or the passive depending on what we are more interested in. In the first sentence, we are more interested in Alfred Hitchcock; in the second sentence, *Psycho* has moved to the beginning of the sentence because we are more interested in the film.

2 *By* and the agent are often omitted in passive sentences if the agent:
   – is not known.
     *My apartment **was robbed** last night.*
   – is not important.
     *This bridge **was built** in 1886.*
   – is obvious.
     *I **was fined** £100 for speeding.*

3 The passive is associated with an impersonal, formal style. It is often used in notices and announcements.
   *Customers **are requested** to refrain from smoking.*
   *It **has been noticed** that reference books **have been removed** from the library.*

4 In informal language, we often use *you*, *we*, and *they* to refer to people in general or to no person in particular. In this way, we can avoid using the passive.
   ***You can buy** stamps in lots of shops, not just the post offices.*
   ***They're building** a new department store in the city centre.*
   ***We speak** English in this shop.*

! Be careful! Many past participles are used as adjectives.
   *I'm very **interested** in modern art.*
   *We were extremely **worried** about you.*
   *I'm **exhausted**! I've been working hard all day.*

2.4 Present Simple and Present Continuous passive

Form

Present Simple Passive   *am/is/are* + past participle
Present Continuous Passive *am/is/are being* + past participle

It	is is being	mended.
They	are are being	

Use

The uses are the same in the passive as in the active.
*My car **is serviced** every six months.* (habit)
*Computers **are used** in all areas of life and work.* (fact that is always true)
*Sorry about the mess. The house **is being redecorated** at the moment.* (activity happening now)

Introduction to past tenses

We use different past tenses to focus on different moments and periods of time in the past.
Look at the diagram. Read the sentences.
When Andrea arrived at work at 9.00 a.m. …

8.30   9.00   9.30   10.00

Her secretary opened the post.
Her secretary was opening the post.
Her secretary had opened the post.

3.1 Past Simple

Form

The form of the Past Simple is the same for all persons.

Positive

I He/She/It We You They	finished left arrived	yesterday. at 3 o'clock. three weeks ago.

Negative

I She They (etc.)	didn't	finish leave	yesterday. at 3 o'clock.

Question

When	did	you he they (etc.)	finish the report? get married?

Short answer

Did you enjoy the meal?	Yes, we did. No, we didn't.

Use

The Past Simple is used to express:

1 a finished action in the past.
   *We **met** in 2000.*
   *I **went** to Manchester last week.*
   *John **left** two minutes ago.*

2 actions that follow each other in a story.
   *Mary **walked** into the room and **stopped**. She **listened** carefully. She **heard** a noise coming from behind the curtain. She **threw** the curtain open, and then she **saw** …*

3 a past situation or habit.
*When I **was** a child, we **lived** in a small house by the sea. Every day I **walked** for miles on the beach with my dog.*
This use is often expressed with *used to*.
*We **used to** live in a small house … I **used to** walk for miles …*

Spelling of verb + -ed

1 Most verbs add -*ed* to the base form of the verb.
worked   wanted   helped   washed

2 When the verb ends in -*e*, add -*d*.
liked   used   hated   cared

3 If the verb has only one syllable, with one vowel + one consonant, double the consonant before adding -*ed*.
stopped   planned   robbed
But we write *cooked*, *seated*, and *moaned* because there are two vowels.

4 The consonant is not doubled if it is -*y* or -*w*.
played   showed

5 In most two-syllable verbs, the end consonant is doubled if the stress is on the second syllable.
pre'ferred   ad'mitted
But we write *'entered* and *'visited* because the stress is on the first syllable.

6 Verbs that end in a consonant + -*y* change the -*y* to -*ied*.
carried   hurried   buried
But we write *enjoyed*, because it ends in a vowel + -*y*.

There are many common irregular verbs.

▶▶ **Irregular verbs p84**

Past Simple and time expressions
Look at the time expressions that are common with the Past Simple.

I met her	last night.
	two days ago.
	yesterday morning.
	in 2001.
	in summer.
	when I was young.

▶ 3.2 Past Continuous

Form

Positive and negative

I He She It	was wasn't	
		working.
We You They	were weren't	

Question

		I she he it	
What	was		doing?
	were	we you they	

Short answer

Were you looking for me?   *Yes, I was./No I wasn't.*
Were they waiting outside?   *Yes, they were./No, they weren't.*

Use
We often use the Past Continuous in sentences with the Past Simple. The Past Continuous refers to longer, background activities, while the Past Simple refers to shorter, completed actions.

The children were playing in the garden …

… when their grandparents arrived.

The Past Continuous is used:

1 to express activities in progress before, and probably after, a particular time in the past.
*At 7 o'clock this morning I **was having** my breakfast.*
*I walked past your house last night. There was an awful lot of noise. What **were** you **doing**?*

2 for descriptions.
*Jan looked beautiful. She **was wearing** a green cotton dress. Her eyes **were shining** in the light of the candles that **were burning** nearby.*

3 to express an interrupted past activity.
*When the phone rang, I **was having** a shower.*
*While we **were playing** tennis, it started to rain.*

4 to express an incomplete activity in the past in order to contrast with the Past Simple that expresses a completed activity.
*I **was reading** a book during the flight. (I didn't finish it.)*
*I **watched** a film during the flight. (the whole film)*

Note
The Past Simple is usually used to express a repeated past habit or situation. But the Past Continuous can be used if the repeated habit becomes a longer setting for something. Compare:
*I **went out with** Jack for ten years.*
*I first met Harry while I **was going out with** Jack.*

▶▶ **Workbook p20**   More information on *while*, *during*, and *for*

▶ 3.3 Past Simple or Past Continuous?

1 Sometimes we can use the Past Simple or the Past Continuous. The Past Simple focuses on past actions as simple facts. The Past Continuous focuses on the duration of past situations and activities. Compare:
A *I didn't see you at the party last night.*
B *No. I **stayed** at home and **watched** football.*

A *I didn't see you at the party last night.*
B *No, I **was watching** football at home.*

2 Questions in the Past Simple and Past Continuous refer to different time periods: the Past Continuous asks about activities before; the Past Simple asks about what happened after.
*When the war broke out, Peter **was studying** medicine at medical school. He **decided** that it was safer to go home to his parents and postpone his studies.*
*What **was** Peter **doing** when the war broke out?*   *He **was studying**.*
*What **did** Peter **do** when the war broke out?*   *He **went** home to his parents.*

3.4 Past Perfect

Perfect means 'before,' so Past Perfect refers to an action in the past that was completed before another action in the past.

Form

The form of the Past Perfect is the same for all persons.

Positive and negative

I You We (etc.)	'd (had) hadn't	seen him before. finished work at 6 o'clock.

Question

Where had	you she they (etc.)	been before?

Short answer

Had he already left?	Yes, he had. No, he hadn't.

Use

1 The Past Perfect is used to make clear that one action in the past happened *before* another action in the past.
*When I got home, I found that someone **had broken** into my apartment and **had stolen** my DVD player, so I called the police.*

PAST ──▶X ──────────▶X ──────▶X ─▶ NOW
          | | |
My DVD player was stolen   I arrived home   I called the police

Action 1: Someone broke into my apartment and stole my DVD player.
Action 2: I got home and called the police.

*I didn't want to go to the theatre with my friends because I'd **seen** the play before.*

PAST ──────▶X ──────────────▶X ──────▶ NOW
              | |
   I saw the play   My friends saw the play

Action 1: I saw the play.
Action 2: My friends went to the theatre to see the play.

2 Notice the difference between the following sentences:
*When I got to the party, Peter **went** home.*
(= First I arrived, then Peter left.)
*When I got to the party, Peter **had gone** home.*
(= First Peter left, then I arrived.)

 3.5 Past tenses in the passive

Form

Past Simple Passive	*was/were* + past participle
Past Continuous Passive	*was/were being* + past participle
Past Perfect Passive	*had been* + past participle

Use

The uses are the same in the passive as in the active.
*The bridge **was built** in 1876.* (finished action in the past)
*The bomb **was being defused** when it exploded.* (interrupted past activity)
*The letter didn't arrive because it **had been sent** to my old address.* (one action before another action in the past)

Introduction to modal verbs

The modal verbs are *can, could, may, might, must, will, would, should, ought to.* They are known as modal auxiliary verbs because they 'help' another verb. (See also Units 1, 5, 8, and 9.)
*I **can** swim.*
*Do you think I **should** go?*

Form

1 There is no *-s* in the third person singular.
*She **can** ski.   He **must** be tired.   It **might** rain.*
2 There is no *do/does/don't/doesn't* in the question or negative.
*What **should** I do?   **Can** I help you?   You **mustn't** steal!*
*He **can't** dance.   I **won't** be a minute.*
3 Modal auxiliary verbs are followed by the infinitive without *to*. The exception is *ought to*.
*You **must** go.   I'll **help** you.   You **ought to** see a doctor.*
4 They have no infinitives and no *-ing* forms. Other expressions are used instead.
*I'd love to **be able to** ski.*
*I hate **having to** get up on cold, winter mornings.*
5 They don't usually have past forms. Instead, we can use them with perfect infinitives:
*You **should have told** me that you can't swim. You **might have** drowned!*

or we use other expressions:
*I **had to** work hard in school.*

Note

Could is used with a past meaning to talk about a general ability.
*I **could** swim when I was six.* (= general ability)

To talk about ability on one specific occasion, we use *was able to/ managed to.*

*The prisoner **was able to/managed to** escape by climbing on to the roof of the prison.*   NOT ~~could escape~~

Use

1 Modal verbs express our attitudes, opinions, and judgments of events. Compare:
'Who's that knocking on the door?'
'It's John.' (This is a fact.)

'Who's that knocking on the door?'
*'It **could/may/might/must/should/can't/'ll** be John.'* (These all express our attitude or opinion.)
2 Each modal verb has at least two meanings. One use of all of them is to express possibility or probability.
*I **must** post this letter!* (= obligation)
*You **must** be tired!* (= deduction, probability)
***Could** you help me?* (= request)
*We **could** go to Spain for our vacation.* (= possibility)
*You **may** go home now.* (= permission)
*'Where's Anna?'   'I'm not sure. She **may** be at work.'* (= possibility)

Modal verbs of obligation and permission

 **4.1 *have (got) to***

Form

Positive and negative

I/You/ We/They	have to don't have to	work hard.
He/She	has to doesn't have to	

Question

Do	I you (etc.)	have to work hard?

Use

Have to is not a modal verb.

1 *Have to* expresses strong obligation. It expresses a general obligation based on a law or rule, or based on the authority of another person. It is impersonal.
   *Children **have to** go to school until they are 16. (a law)*
   *Mum says you **have to** clean your room before you go out. (mother's order)*

2 *Have got to* is common in British English but it is more informal than *have to*.
   *I've **got to** go now. See you!*
   *Don't go to bed late. We've **got to** get up early tomorrow.*
   *'Go and tidy your room.' '**Have I got to**?' 'Yes, you **have**!'*

3 *Have to* expresses a general repeated obligation.
   *I always **have to** tell my parents where I'm going.*
   Have got to expresses an obligation on one particular occasion.
   *I've **got to** get up early tomorrow to catch a train.*

 ***can*** and ***be allowed to***

Form

Affirmative and negative

I/You/ We/They	can/can't are allowed to aren't allowed to	park here.
He/She	can/can't is allowed to isn't allowed to	

Question

Can	I/you/we etc.		
Am	I	allowed to	park here?
Are	you		
Is	he		

Use

Can is a modal verb.

Can and *be allowed to* express permission. *Can* is more informal and usually spoken.
*You **can** borrow my bike, but you **can't** have the car. I need it.*
*They **can't** come in here with those muddy shoes!*
*You**'re allowed to** get married when you're 16.*
***Are** we **allowed to** use a dictionary for this test?*
*He **isn't allowed to** park here.*

 **4.2 *should*, *ought to*, and *must***

Form

Should, ought to, and *must* are modal verbs.

I/You/We/They He/She/ It	should/shouldn't ought to / ought not to must	work hard.

Use

1 *Should* and *ought to* express mild obligation, suggestions, or advice. They express what, in the speaker's opinion, is the right or best thing to do. We often use them with *I think/don't think …* .
   *You're always asking me for money. I think you **should** spend less.*
   *You **shouldn't** sit so close to the television! It's bad for your eyes.*
   *You **ought to** be more careful with your money.*

2 *Should I/she/we … ?* is possible. We often use *Do you think … ?*
   ***Should I** try to eat less?*
   *Do you think **I should** see a doctor?*

3 *Must*, like *have to*, expresses strong obligation. *Must* expresses an obligation that involves the speaker's opinion. It is personal.
   *I **must** get my hair cut. (This is me talking to me.)*
   *You **must** go and visit your grandmother. (A parent talking to a child.)*

4 *Must* is also associated with a formal, written style.
   *All visitors **must** show proper ID. (Sign in the lobby of an office building)*
   *Books **must** be returned on or before the due date. (Instructions in a library)*

have to and *must*, *don't have to* and *mustn't*

1 *Have to* and *must* are sometimes interchangeable.
   *I **must** be home by midnight.   I **have to** be home by midnight.*
   But *have to* is used more often than *must*. If you are unsure which to use, it is probably safer to use *have to*.

2 *Must I … ?* is possible, but question forms with *have to* are more common.
   *Do I **have to** do what you say, or can I do what I want?*

3 *Have to* has all forms; *must* does not.
   *I **had to** work until midnight last night. (Past)*
   *You'll **have to** study hard when you go to college. (Future)*
   *She's a millionaire. She's never **had to** do any work. (Present Perfect)*
   *I hate **having to** get up on cold, winter mornings. (-ing form)*
   *If you were a nurse, you would **have to** wear a uniform. (Infinitive)*

4 *Don't have to* and *mustn't* are completely different.
   Don't have to expresses absence of obligation – you can but it isn't necessary.
   *Some people iron their socks, but you **don't have to**. I think it's a waste of time.*
   *When you go into a shop, you **don't have to** buy something. You can just look.*
   Mustn't expresses negative obligation – it is very important not to do something.
   *You **mustn't** steal other people's things. It's wrong.*
   *You **mustn't** drive if you've been drinking. You could kill someone!*

▶▶ **Workbook p28**   Further practice of *must* and *have to*

4.3 Making requests: *can*, *could*, *will*, and *would*

1 There are many ways of making requests in English.

Can Could Will Would	you	help me, please? pass the salt, please?

Would you mind helping me, please?

Can Could	I	speak to you, please? ask you a question?

Do you mind if I open the window?
Would you mind if I opened the window?

Can, *could*, *will*, and *would* are all modal verbs.

2 *Could* is a little more formal; *can* is a little more familiar. *Could I … ?* and *Could you … ?* are very useful because they can be used in many different situations.

3 Here are some ways of responding to requests:
   A *Excuse me! Could you help me?*
   B *Sure.*
   Of course.
   Well, I'm afraid I'm a little busy right now.
   A *Would you mind if I opened the window?*
   B *No, not at all.*
   No, that's fine.
   Well, I'm a little cold, actually.

4.4 Making offers: *will* and *shall/should*

1 *Will* and *shall/should* are used to express offers. They are both modal verbs.

2 The contracted form of *will* is used to express an intention, decision, or offer made at the moment of speaking.
   Come over after work. I'll cook dinner for you.
   'It's Jane's birthday today.' 'Is it? I'll buy her some flowers.'
   Give him your suitcase. He'll carry it for you.
   Don't worry about catching the bus. Dave'll give you a lift.
   Give it back or we'll call the police!

   In many languages, this idea is often expressed by a present tense, but in English this is wrong.
   I'll give you my number.   NOT   ~~I give you my number.~~
   I'll carry your suitcase.   NOT   ~~I carry your suitcase.~~

   Other uses of *will* are dealt with in Unit 5.

3 *Shall / Should …?* is used in questions with the first person, *I* and *we*. It expresses an offer, a suggestion, or a request for advice.
   *'**Shall** I carry your bag for you?' 'That's very kind. Thank you.'*
   *'**Shall** we go out for a meal tonight?' 'Mmm. I'd love to.'*
   *'What **shall** we do? We haven't got any money.' 'We could ask Dad.'*

   We use **should** to make an informal suggestion.
   *What **should** we have for dinner?*
   *What **should** we do tonight?*

UNIT 5

Introduction to future forms

There is no future tense in English as there is in many European languages. However, English has several forms that can refer to the future. Three of these are *will*, *going to*, and the Present Continuous.
I'll see you later. (will)
We're going to see a movie tonight. Do you want to come? (going to)
I'm seeing the doctor tomorrow evening. (Present Continuous)

The difference between them is *not* about near or distant future, or about certainty. The speaker chooses a future form depending on how the speaker sees the future event. Is it a plan, a decision, an intention, an offer, a prediction, or an arrangement? This is the important question to ask when choosing a future form. There is more about this in **Use** below.

5.1 *will / going to* and the Present Continuous

Form

Positive and negative

I He They	'll won't	help you. watch TV tonight.
I'm / I'm not She's / She isn't We're / We aren't	going to	
I'm / I'm not He's / He isn't You're / You aren't	catching the 10 o'clock train.	

Question

What time	will you are you going to	arrive?
	are you meeting the manager?	

Note
We avoid saying *going to come* or *going to go*.
We're coming tomorrow.
When are you going home?

Use

Plans, decisions, and intentions (*will* and *going to*)

will
Will is used as a modal auxiliary verb to express a decision, intention, or offer made at the moment of speaking. We saw this use in Unit 4. (See 4.4.) Remember that you can't use the present tense for this use.
I'll have the steak, please.   NOT   ~~I have the steak.~~
I'll see you tomorrow. Bye!   NOT   ~~I see you tomorrow.~~
Give me a call sometime. We'll go out for coffee.
'Jeff, there's someone at the door!' 'OK, I'll get it.'

going to
Going to is used to express a future plan, decision, or intention made before the moment of speaking.
*When I grow up, I'm **going to be** a doctor.*
*Jane and Peter **are going to get married** after they graduate.*
*We're **going to paint** this room blue.*

Facts and predictions (*will* and *going to*)

will
The most common use of *will* is as an auxiliary verb to show future time. It expresses a future fact or prediction. It is called the pure future or the Future Simple.
*We'll **be** away for two weeks.*
*Those flowers **won't grow** under the tree. It's too dark.*
*Our love **will last** forever.*
*You'll **be** sick if you eat all those sweets!*

Will for a prediction can be based more on an opinion than a fact.
*I don't think Laura **will do** very well in her exam. She doesn't do any work.*
*I am convinced that inflation **will fall** to three per cent next year.*

going to
Going to can also express a prediction, especially when it is based on a present fact. There is evidence now that something is certain to happen.
*She's **going to have** a baby.* (We can see she's pregnant.)
*Our team **is going to win** the match.* (It's four–nil, and there are only five minutes left to play.)
*It **isn't going to rain** today.* (Look at that beautiful blue sky.)

Note
Sometimes there is no difference between *will* and *going to*.

This government	will ruin is going to ruin	the country with its stupid economic policies.

Arrangements (Present Continuous)

The Present Continuous can be used to express a future arrangement between people. It usually refers to the near future.
*We're **going** out with Jeremy tonight.*
*I'm **having** my hair cut tomorrow.*
*What **are** we **having** for lunch?*

Think of the things you might put in your diary to remind you of what you are doing over the next few days and weeks. These are the kinds of events that are often expressed by the Present Continuous for the future. The verbs express some kind of activity or movement.
*I'm **meeting** Peter tonight.*
*The Taylors **are coming** for dinner.*
*I'm **seeing** the doctor in the morning.*

Remember that you can't use the present tense for this use.
*We're **going** to a party on Saturday night.*
NOT ~~We go to a party on Saturday night.~~
*We're **catching** the 10 o'clock train.*
NOT ~~We catch the 10 o'clock train.~~
*What **are** you **doing** this evening?*
NOT ~~What do you do this evening?~~

Sometimes there is no difference between an agreed arrangement (Present Continuous) and an intention (*going to*).

We're going to get We're getting	married in the spring.

Introduction to *like*

Like can be a verb or a preposition.
Like as a verb can be followed by *-ing* or *to*, sometimes with a change in meaning.
*I **like** going out at the weekend.* (general enjoyment)
*I **like** to sit in a hot bath and read.* (habits and preferences)

Like as a verb has a person as the subject:
*I **like** modern art.*
*I don't **like** the way he looks at me.*
*Do you **like** fish?*
*Would you **like** a drink?*

Like as a preposition has an object after it:
*She's wearing a hat **like** mine.*
*He's nothing **like** his father.*
*That sounds **like** the postman.*
*You're behaving **like** children.*
*This new girlfriend of his – what's she **like**?*

6.1 *What ... like?*

What is/are/was/were ... like? is used to ask about the permanent nature of people and things. It asks for a description or an impression or a comparison.
***What's** the health service **like** in your country?*
***What are** the new students **like**?*

🛈 Be careful!

1 With a description or an impression, we do not use *like* in the answer.
    *What's London **like**?*   *It's quite big, and it's very interesting.*
                          NOT ~~It's like quite big ...~~
    *What's Amanda **like**?*   *She's tall, attractive, and very funny.*
                          NOT ~~She's like tall ...~~

2 With a comparison, we can use *like* in the answer. Here, *like* means *similar to / the same as*.
    *What's London **like**?*   *It's **like** New York, but without the tall buildings.* (= It's similar to ...)
    *What's Amanda's daughter **like**?*
                          *She's just **like** Amanda.*
                          (= She's the same as ...)

▶▶ **Workbook p39**   *Like* and *as*

6.2 *How ...?*

1 *How ... ?* is used to ask about the present condition of something that can change.
    ***How's** work these days?*   *It's better than last year.*
    ***How** was the traffic this morning?*   *It was worse than usual.*
    To ask about the weather, we can use both questions.

How's the weather What's the weather like	where you are?

2 *How ... ?* is also used to ask about people's health and happiness. Compare:
    How's Peter?   *He's fine.*
    What's Peter like?   *He's a nice guy. He's quite tall, has dark hair ...*

3 *How ... ?* is also used to ask about people's reactions and feelings.
    ***How's** your meal?*
    ***How's** your new job?*

6.3 *How ...?* or *What ... like?*

Sometimes we can use *What ... like?* or *How ... ?*, but they aren't the same. *What ... like?* asks for an objective description. *How ... ?* asks for personal feelings. Compare:

How's the party?   *It's great!*
What's the party like?   *It's very noisy, but there's lots to eat and drink.*

6.4 Verb + *-ing* or infinitive

▶▶ **Verb patterns p85**

6.5 Relative clauses

1   Relative clauses are used to tell us which person or thing we are talking about. They make it possible to give more information about the person or thing being spoken about.
   The boy has gone to the beach. (Which boy?)
   *The boy **who lives next door** has gone to the beach.*
   The book is very good. (Which book?)
   *The book **that I bought yesterday** is very good.*
   This is a photo of the hotel. (Which hotel?)
   *This is a photo of the hotel **where we stayed**.*

2   We use *who* to refer to people (and we can also use *that*).
   *The book is about a girl **who** marries a millionaire.*

   We use *that* to refer to things (and we can also use *which*).
   *What was the name of the horse **that** won the race?*

3   When *who* or *that* is the object of a relative clause, it can be left out.
   *The person **you need to talk to** is on holiday.*
   *The book **I bought yesterday** is very good.*

   But when *who* or *that* is the subject of a relative clause, it must be included.
   *I like people **who are kind and considerate**.*
   *I want a computer **that is easy to use**.*

4   *Which* can be used to refer to the whole previous sentence or idea.
   *I passed my driving test on my first attempt, **which surprised everyone**.*
   *Jane can't come to the party, **which is a shame**.*

5   We use *whose* to refer to someone's possessions.
   *That's the woman **whose dog ran away**.*
   *That's the man **whose wife won the lottery**.*

6   We can use *where* to refer to places.
   *The hotel **where we stayed** was right on the beach.*
   *We went back to the place **where we first met**.*

6.6 Participles

Participles after a noun define and identify in the same way as relative clauses.
*That woman **driving** the red Porsche is my aunt.*
*The men **seen** outside were probably the thieves.*

Pairwork activities

UNIT 1 *p9*

PRACTICE
An amazing thing happened!

Student A
Ask and answer questions to complete the information about Kaori Sato.

> *Where was Kaori Sato born?*

> *In Osaka. How many films has she made?*

> *Over forty. How long … ?*

KAORI SATO
United Nations Goodwill Ambassador

Kaori Sato was born in __Osaka, Japan__ (*Where?*), in 1956. She is a famous film star and has made over forty films.

She has been a UN Goodwill Ambassador for _____ (*How long?*). Her special interest is children's health and education. She goes to Africa _____ (*How often?*), and she visits schools and hospitals. She has raised _____ (*How much money?*) from people in Japan. As a Goodwill Ambassador, she is paid just $1 a year.

Her father was a famous _____ (*What/do?*). Kaori went to university in Tokyo, then studied _____ (*What?*) at the Tokyo Theatre School. She has also written seven best-selling books.

She is married, and has _____ (*How many?*) children. They are both at university, studying languages.

UNIT 3 *p25*

PRACTICE
Getting information

Student A
Ask and answer questions to complete the story.

> *Where did Wanda and Roy go on holiday?*

> *They went to Florida. What did they do every day?*

> *They went swimming and lay in the sun. Where … ?*

THE TALE OF TWO WAVES
A TRUE STORY

Last summer, Wanda and Roy went on holiday to _____ Florida _____ (*Where?*). Every day, they went swimming and lay in the sun.

One morning, they were _____ (*Where?*), swimming in the sea, when a huge wave knocked Wanda's expensive Italian sunglasses into the water. Wanda was very upset because _____ (*Why?*).

The next day, they were sunbathing on the same beach and Wanda was wearing _____ (*What?*), when suddenly there was another huge wave, which totally covered Wanda. She was _____ (*How … feel?*), but then she looked down and to her amazement, she saw the expensive sunglasses that she had lost the day before.

PRACTICE

Getting information

Student B

Ask and answer questions to complete the information about Kaori Sato.

> *Where was Kaori Sato born?*

> *In Osaka. How many films has she made?*

> *Over forty. How long … ?*

KAORI SATO
United Nations Goodwill Ambassador

Kaori Sato was born in Osaka, Japan, in 1956. She is a famous film star and has made __over forty__ (*How many?*) films.

She has been a UN Goodwill Ambassador for 20 years. Her special interest is _____ (*What?*). She goes to Africa every year, and she visits _____ (*What?*). She has raised $25 million from people in Japan. As a Goodwill Ambassador, she is paid _____ (*How much?*).

Her father was a famous painter. Kaori went to university in _____ (*Where?*), then studied drama at the Tokyo Theatre School. She has also written _____ (*How many?*) best-selling books.

She is married, and has two children. They are both at university, studying _____ (*What?*).

UNIT 3 *p25*

PRACTICE

An amazing thing happened!

Student B

Ask and answer questions to complete the story.

> *Where did Wanda and Roy go on holiday?*

> *They went to Florida. What did they do every day?*

> *They went swimming and lay in the sun. Where … ?*

THE TALE OF TWO WAVES
A TRUE STORY

Last summer, Wanda and Roy went on holiday to Florida. Every day, they __went swimming and lay in the sun__ (*What … do?*).

One morning, they were at the beach near their hotel, swimming in the sea, when a huge wave _____ (*What … do?*). Wanda was very upset because Roy had given her the sunglasses for her birthday.

The next day, they were sunbathing _____ (*Where?*) and Wanda was wearing a new, cheap pair of sunglasses, when suddenly there was another huge wave, which _____ (*What … do?*). She was furious, but then she looked down and to her amazement, she saw _____ (*What?*).

VOCABULARY

Talking about you

1 Work with a partner. List the following information.

- the name of a restaurant where you had a memorable meal
- the name of a city, town, or village that you have visited and that you would like to visit again
- the name of a relative, friend, or colleague who is important to you

Choose names of people and places that your partner does not know.

2 Exchange lists with your partner.
Ask and answer questions to find out about
the places and people your partner listed.

> *Where was the restaurant?*

> *What was the food like?*

3 Report back to the class about one of the names your partner wrote.

Irregular verbs

Base form	Past Simple	Past participle
be	was/were	been
beat	beat	beaten
become	became	become
begin	began	begun
bend	bent	bent
bite	bit	bitten
blow	blew	blown
break	broke	broken
bring	brought	brought
build	built	built
buy	bought	bought
can	could	been able
catch	caught	caught
choose	chose	chosen
come	came	come
cost	cost	cost
cut	cut	cut
dig	dug	dug
do	did	done
draw	drew	drawn
dream	dreamed/dreamt	dreamed/dreamt
drink	drank	drunk
drive	drove	driven
eat	ate	eaten
fall	fell	fallen
feed	fed	fed
feel	felt	felt
fight	fought	fought
find	found	found
fit	fit	fit
fly	flew	flown
forget	forgot	forgotten
forgive	forgave	forgiven
freeze	froze	frozen
get	got	got
give	gave	given
go	went	been/gone
grow	grew	grown
hang	hanged/hung	hanged/hung
have	had	had
hear	heard	heard
hide	hid	hidden
hit	hit	hit
hold	held	held
hurt	hurt	hurt
keep	kept	kept
kneel	knelt	knelt
know	knew	known
lay	laid	laid
lead	led	led
learn	learned/learnt	learned/learnt

Base form	Past Simple	Past participle
leave	left	left
lend	lent	lent
let	let	let
lie	lay	lain
light	lighted/lit	lighted/lit
lose	lost	lost
make	made	made
mean	meant	meant
meet	met	met
must	had to	had to
pay	paid	paid
put	put	put
read /ri:d/	read /red/	read /red/
ride	rode	ridden
ring	rang	rung
rise	rose	risen
run	ran	run
say	said	said
see	saw	seen
sell	sold	sold
send	sent	sent
set	set	set
shake	shook	shaken
shine	shone	shone
shoot	shot	shot
show	showed	shown
shut	shut	shut
sing	sang	sung
sink	sank	sunk
sit	sat	sat
sleep	slept	slept
slide	slid	slid
speak	spoke	spoken
spend	spent	spent
spoil	spoiled/spoilt	spoiled/spoilt
spread	spread	spread
stand	stood	stood
steal	stole	stolen
stick	stuck	stuck
swim	swam	swum
take	took	taken
teach	taught	taught
tear	tore	torn
tell	told	told
think	thought	thought
throw	threw	thrown
understand	understood	understood
wake	woke	woken
wear	wore	worn
win	won	won
write	wrote	written

Verb patterns

Verbs + *-ing*	
adore can't stand don't mind enjoy finish look forward to	doing swimming cooking

Note

We often use the verb *go* + *-ing* for sports and activities.

I go swimming every day.
I go shopping on weekends.

Verbs + *to* + infinitive	
agree choose dare decide expect forget help hope learn manage need offer promise refuse seem want would hate would like would love would prefer	to do to come to cook

Notes

1 *Help* and *dare* can be used without *to*.
  *We **helped clean up** the kitchen.*
  *They didn't **dare disagree** with him.*

2 *Have to* for obligation.
  *I **have to wear** a uniform.*

3 *Used to* for past habits.
  *I **used to smoke**, but I quit last year.*

Verbs + sb + *to* + infinitive		
advise allow ask beg encourage expect help invite need order remind tell want warn would like	me him them someone	to do to go to come

Note

Help can be used without *to*.
  *I **helped** him **do** the dishes.*

Verbs + sb + infinitive (no *to*)		
help let make	her us	do

Notes

1 *To* is used with *make* in the passive.
  *We were **made to work** hard.*

2 *Let* cannot be used in the passive. *Allowed to* is used instead.
  *She was **allowed to leave**.*

Verbs + *-ing* or *to* + infinitive (with little or no change in meaning)	
begin continue hate like love prefer start	doing to do

Verbs + *-ing* or *to* + infinitive (with a change in meaning)	
remember stop try	doing to do

Notes

1 *I **remember posting** the letter.*
   (= I have a memory now of a past action: posting the letter.)

   *I **remembered to post** the letter.*
   (= I reminded myself to post the letter. I didn't forget.)

2 *I **stopped drinking** coffee.*
   (= I gave up the habit.)

   *I **stopped to drink** a coffee.*
   (= I stopped doing something else in order to have a cup of coffee.)

3 *I **tried to sleep**.*
   (= I wanted to sleep, but it was difficult.)

   *I **tried counting** sheep and **drinking** a glass of warm milk.*
   (= These were possible ways of getting to sleep.)

OXFORD
UNIVERSITY PRESS

Great Clarendon Street, Oxford OX2 6DP

Oxford University Press is a department of the University of Oxford.

It furthers the University's objective of excellence in research, scholarship, and education by publishing worldwide in

Oxford New York

Auckland Bangkok Buenos Aires Cape Town Chennai Dar es Salaam Delhi Hong Kong Istanbul Karachi Kolkata Kuala Lumpur Madrid Melbourne Mexico City Mumbai Nairobi São Paulo Shanghai Taipei Tokyo Toronto

Oxford and Oxford English are registered trade marks of Oxford University Press in the UK and in certain other countries

© Oxford University Press 2003

The moral rights of the author have been asserted

Database right Oxford University Press (maker)

First published 2003

ISBN 0 19 438750 X Complete edition
ISBN 0 19 438751 8 Student's Book A
ISBN 0 19 438752 6 Student's Book B

Printed in China

Acknowledgements

The authors and publisher are grateful to those who have given permission to reproduce the following extracts and adaptations of copyright material:

p16 'College grad loves life as a $60,000-a-year paperboy' by Philip Smith, The National Enquirer 23 January 2001. Reproduced by permission of American Media Inc.
p18 Information about The Clown Doctor. Reproduced by permission of Theodora Children's Trust.
p68 Amnesty International information and Logo © Amnesty International Publications, 1 Easton Street, London WC1X 0DW www.amnesty.org . Reproduced by permission.
p68 Information about WWF. Reproduced by permission of WWF-UK.
p82 Information about Dennis Woodruff. Reproduced by permission.

p84 Information about Andrea Levitt. Reproduced by permission.
p98 Information about Jane Banner. Reproduced by permission.
p99 'Twelve Songs IX' from Collected Poems by W.H. Auden. Reproduced by permission of Faber and Faber Ltd.
p100 My Way. Original Words by Gilles Thibaut. English Translation by Paul Anka. Music by Claude Francois and Jacques Revaux © 1967 Editions Jeune Musique SARL and Warner/Chappell Music, France. (50%) Warner/Chappell Music Ltd., London W6 8BS. (50%) Sony Music Ltd. Reproduced by permission of International Music Publications Ltd. and Sony Music Publishing (UK) Ltd. All Rights Reserved.

Illustrations by:
Jamel Akib/Illustration pp114/115, Francis Blake/Three in a Box p89; Marc Burckhardt p22/23; Kasia Charko p58; Mark Duffin pp25, 32, 44; Hannah Firmin/ Illustration p62; Jacey/Debut Art p40; Karen Minot p9; Joerg Saupe/Illustration pp22, 49, 70, 78, 86; Carlotta Tormey p59; Harry Venning pp6, 14, 30, 38, 46, 54, 62; Katherine Walker pp 49, 60, 73, 75; Sam Wilson pp17, 65

Commissioned photography by:
Dennis Kitchen Studio; Jodi Waxman/OUP pp8, 9, 12, 15, 32, 38, 39, 41, 46, 47, 48, 51, 55, 81, 82, 84, 85, 86, 88; Mark Mason; pp27 (books – 'For Whom the Bell Tolls' and 'A Farewell to Arms' book covers used by permission of the Random House Group Limited), 28 (books and DVDs – 'Captain Corelli's Mandolin' book cover used by permission of the Random House Group Limited; 'Harry Potter and the Philosopher's Stone' book cover used with kind permission from Bloomsbury Publishing and the illustrator, Thomas Taylor), 53 (labels); Chris King; pp75 (grown up father and daughter), 65, 79, 80, 96, 97, 101 (woman asking for directions), 103 (writing paper and pencil)

We would also like to thank the following for permission to reproduce photographs:
Agence France Presse pp11 (Olympic flame), 34 (Muslim women); AgeFotostock pp69 (P.Coll/Maria and Paul), 77 (P.Coll/Rose); AKG London p92 Auguste Rodin, (The Thinker, bronze sculpture, 1889); Amnesty International p68 (logo); The Anthony Blake Photo Library p153 (pizza restaurant); Artcars/www.artcaragency.com p83 (H.Blank/ Dennis Woodruff); BAA Aviation Photo Library p53 (airport sign); The Bridgeman Art Library p26 (Pablo Picasso, Guernica, 1937, Museo Nacional Centro de Arte Reina Sofia, Madrid, © Succession Picasso/DACS 2003); Bubbles Photo Library p60 (J.Woodcock/exams), (J.Powell/café); © Daily Record, Glasgow p98 (group photo); Claudia Carlson p12; Corbis pp6 (K.Weatherly/ Olympic flag), 7 (Bettmann/John Lennon), 14 (M.Barrymore/two women drinking coffee), (D.Modricker/ bowling), 29 (C.Penn/sitting on steps), 34 (C.Bissell/ business lunch), (P.Ward/large family meal), 37 (P.Schermeister), 42 (L.Kennedy/Ice Hotel), (S.Warren/ The Burj Al-Arab), (S.Balfour/Gallo Images/Baobab Rivers Lodge), 43 (D.S.Robbins/hotel bedroom), 45 (M.McQueen/ferry), 52 (B.Krist/NY street scene), 56 (R.Holmes/hurricane), (M.Brennan/boxers), 59 (D.Jones/ trapeze artist), 61 (R.Hutchings/retired man), 63 (R.Juno/ lemons), 69 (R.Ressmeyer/animal rescue), 81 (S.Maze), 90 (D.S.Robbins/bristlecone pine), 91 (Bettmann/Uncle Sam), 100 (Bettmann), 83 (F.Seguin/ footballers); Corel p109; Getty Images pp6-7 (D.Scott/ aeroplane), 10 (H.Kingsnorth/internet café), 13 (B.Ayres), 14 (Antonio Mo/three young people laughing), 20 (A.Myers/ snowboarding), (D.Epperson/fishing), (W.R.Sallaz/ basketball), (P.Grumann/football), (C.Bissell/aerobics), (J.Kelly/mountain biking), (S.McClymont/joggers),

(A.Marsland/Yoga), 21 (B.Ayres/Mary), (J.F.Causse/ Jenny), (G.Lepp/Thomas), 24 (M.Malyszko), 28 (S.Mason/ four people at table), 29 (Piecework Productions/two women talking in street), (S.Cohen/man with glasses talking), 31 (A.Sacks/supermarket), (P.Cade/man and car), 32-33 (J.Wang /Thailand), 34 (K.Usami/business card exchange), 36 (A.Weinbrecht/people at table in Japan), (M.Miyatake/sushi), 43 (R.McVay /Karen Saunders), 45 (V.C.L./Tipp Howell/man in hotel), 53, 74 (A.Pistolesi/London taxi), 55 (A.Incrocci/Geneva), 61 (R.McVay/man on phone), 62 (R.Davies/people in rain), 64 (J.Lamb/black woman), (D.Boissavy/boy), (E.Holub/older man), 72 (C.M.Rogers/Carl), (T.Anderson/Andy), 74 (A. Pistolesi), 77 (D.Healey/ Louisa), 86 (P.Gridley/Toronto), 91 (Z.Kaluzny/old women), 94-5 (D.Oliver), 99 (F.Seifert), 101 (R.Lockyer/ man), 116 (J.Cummins), 83 (S.Egan/hillside village), (Creaps/women on sofa); Getty Images/Foodpix p47 (Burke/Triolo Productions/food); Getty Images/Sport p20 (D.McNamara/volleyball); Hulton Archive/Getty Images pp26 (Picasso portrait), 27 (Hemingway); Index Stock pp10-11 (J.Halaska/medical researcher), 11 (NASA/Space Shuttle), 14 (C.Freelance/two young boys hugging), 30 (D.Frazier), 50 (Great American Stock/ large Pepperoni pizza), 51 (SW Production/pizza delivery), 53 (H.Kaiser/NY skyline), 59 (S.Dunwell Photography Inc/ironworker), 61 (B.Lai/woman on phone), 69 (M.Cate/soup kitchen), 70 (M. Giolas), 72 (J.Fly/snow scene), 83 (M.Diamond/Hollywood), 90 (L.Stone/dog), (K.Su/Great Wall of China); Andrew Itkoff p58 (hurricane hunter): Katz Pictures p68 (A.Patrick/World Food Programme); Larry Luxner/ Luxner News Inc. p11 (Tourists at Macchu Picchu); Midweststock p11 (K.Sink/farm); National Enquirer p16; Courtesy of The Nobel Foundation p117 (painting of Alfred Nobel by Emil Österman); PA Photos pp50 (EPA/giant pizza Naples), 56 (EPA/police), (D.Jones/car workers), 67 (J.Giles/family), (PA/couple and cheque), (S.Rousseau/couple and car), 87 (EPA), 155 (W.Conran/ Madonna), 156 (W.Conran/Madonna); PhotoDisc pp51 (C Squared Studios/pizza in letter O), 64 (A.Morgan/ young man), 93 (R.McVay), 119 (J.Hollingworth); Photofusion p52 (R.Roberts/London Eye), 64 (P.Baldesare/white woman); Photonica pp11 (M.Steinbacher/person in rock formation), 29 (Johner/ couple at a table); Courtesy of Pizza Hut Inc. p50 (Wirepix/pizza in space); Powerstock Superstock pp25 (couple), 81 (couple), 82 (couple); Reuters p56 (Nobel Prize), 91 (disaster); Robert Harding Picture Library pp89; 90-91 (earth); Roberstock.com p91 (L.Smith/plane); Sally & Richard Greenhill pp45 (underground), 154 (Simon and baby), (Simon and siblings), 155 (couple with two children), (four adults), (large group); Science Photo Library p101 (T.McHugh/Diplodocus); Science & Society Picture Library p6 (Science Museum/glasses); Scotland in Focus p98 (R.G.Elliott/landscape); Still Digital p20 (Still Moving Picture Company/golf); Still Pictures pp69 (R.Giling/ Linear/African child), (M.Harvey/rhino); By kind permission of Theodora Children's Trust, www.theodora.org pp18, 19; WWF/ www.panda.org p68 (logo); www.artcaragency.com p83 (H.Blank/Dennis Woodruff); Zefa pp33 (R.James /grandmother), 101 (P.Leonard/grandmother), 83 (Visual Media/ G.Rossenbach/town fountain); Janie Zohrer; p74 (young father and daughter)

Although every effort has been made to trace and contact copyright holders before publication, this has not been possible in some cases. We apologize for any apparent infringement of copyright and if notified, the publisher will be pleased to rectify any errors or omissions at the earliest opportunity.